OUR FATHERS HAVE TOLD US

*The Story of
the Founding of Methodism in
Western Pennsylvania*

JACOB SIMPSON PAYTON

THE RUTER PRESS
CINCINNATI
1938

Copyright, 1938
by
JACOB SIMPSON PAYTON

To the Memory of
WILLIAM FRANCIS CONNER

INTRODUCTION

THE Historical Society of the Pittsburgh Conference was organized in 1882. Therefore, more than half a century ago there were members of the Pittsburgh Conference who had an appreciation of the origin of Methodism within the original boundaries of the Conference. They also looked forward to a time when the historical records containing an account of the rise of Methodism in Western Pennsylvania and adjacent territory would become the prized possession of Methodist ministers who would carry on the work so nobly and heroically begun by the fathers. The securing of historical data, definitely documented, has been an arduous and difficult task, for the founders of Methodism in this section were too busily engaged in making history to commit to writing an account of their unselfish and sacrificial labors.

Although Methodism was introduced into Western Pennsylvania in the year 1784, the Pittsburgh Conference was not organized until 1825. Much of the history of the Pittsburgh Conference centers about Redstone Circuit, where the work of the Methodist Episcopal Church first took denominational form beyond the Pennsylvania Alleghenies. A history of "Old Redstone" is in reality a history of the beginning of Methodism in a section of our country that has made an unexcelled contribution to the religious, economic, and political life of the nation. Such men as Bishops Asbury and Whatcoat and such pioneer preachers as Asa Shinn, Thornton Fleming, James Quinn, William Knox, and many others worthy of special mention counted not their lives dear unto themselves in order that they might bring men and women to a saving knowledge of Christ.

In recent years much much valuable historical data has been discovered and among the members of the Conference there has been a noticeable awakening of interest in the development of Methodism in this section. At the session of the Pittsburgh Conference held in the South Avenue Methodist Episcopal Church, Wilkinsburg, Pennsylvania, September, 1937, a commission was raised and instructed to plan for a fitting celebration of the organization of the Conference at the session to be held in historic Uniontown on September 27, 1938.

In planning the celebration the commission decided that one of the most important contributions to future Methodism that could possibly be made would be a new and modern history of the Methodist Episcopal Church in Western Pennsylvania. Of all the members of the Conference, there was just one man qualified for this important task. It was upon the urgent and unanimous invitation of the commission that the Reverend Jacob Simpson Payton, D.D., Editor of *The National Methodist Press*, consented to write the history.

Dr. Payton has chosen as the title of the volume, Our Fathers Have Told Us. The volume contains a history of Methodism in Western Pennsylvania from the time of its introduction in 1784 up to the year 1800. The author has left nothing undone in the writing of this brief history. The thoroughness with which this work has been carried out is characteristic of the author, and the entire volume is intensively documented.

In view of the immense amount of work that has

already been done and because of the valuable material secured in the preparation of this volume, we express the hope that at some future time Dr. Payton may see his way clear to continue his studies in this important field and give to the Church a complete history of Methodism in Western Pennsylvania.

Inasmuch as the three great bodies of Methodists have voted to unite, this history, which commemorates the sesquicentennial of the Pittsburgh Conference, takes on additional historic interest and becomes all the more valuable to the Pittsburgh Conference and to the larger and newer Methodist Church.

A. W. LEONARD.

September 3, 1938

FOREWORD

IT IS an aphorism that those who make history seldom record it. Of the Methodist circuit-riders who, beginning with 1784, helped fashion the civilization in the Valley of the Ohio beyond the Allegheny Mountains, this was particularly true. Many of them acted under a divine compulsion, which prevented any deviation from the pursuit of their soul-saving ministry. A few may have been too unlettered to chronicle the events of which they were a part. Others no doubt felt their contribution too insignificant to record. John Cooper moved along dim trails with the ease of a Fremont. Lasley Matthews could have written a wilderness Baedeker. The stirring scenes, however, went unreported. The high hours along with their heroes have become all but legendary.

This little volume is an attempt to recover out of a day long gone certain facts either lost or forgotten; to set the old circuit-riders cantering off to their preaching places, and to lead forward into clearer view certain figures long enshrouded in the mists of the years. In this undertaking so many authors and so many friends have come to my help that, deserving of public acknowledgment as their services are, their names of necessity must go unmentioned.

The period covered in these pages extends from 1784, when Methodist preachers were first appointed to the Redstone Circuit in Western Pennsylvania, to the year 1800. The story is confined largely to that section of Pennsylvania and West Virginia included within the present bounds of the Pittsburgh Conference. Inasmuch as this period falls within what has come to be regarded as the heroic age of Methodism, it has been necessary to guard against an overstatement of the worth and services of these men. We have attempted to hang out the banners for the saints in their passing, but to lower the flags to half-mast when a failure has come into view. Withal they were a glorious company.

JACOB SIMPSON PAYTON.

Washington, D. C.

CONTENTS

INTRODUCTION, BISHOP ADNA WRIGHT LEONARD	5
FOREWORD	9

CHAPTER I
THEY GO UP TO POSSESS THE LAND . . . 13

CHAPTER II
OUTPOSTS OF ZION 24

CHAPTER III
THEY DELIVERED THE FAITH 36

CHAPTER IV
MORE OF THE LORD'S HORSEMEN ARRIVE . . 43

CHAPTER V
ALL ROADS LEAD FROM UNIONTOWN . . . 58

CHAPTER VI
WHEN FAITH FLAMED IN THE DARKNESS . . 73

CHAPTER VII
"SO MIGHTILY GREW THE WORD OF GOD AND PROSPERED" 80

CHAPTER VIII
LENGTHENING TRAILS AND RECEDING HORIZONS   95

CHAPTER IX
A STRONG MAN COMES OVER THE MOUNTAINS 111

CHAPTER X
THE CURTAIN FALLS ON A CENTURY OF DRAMA 128

INDEX 137

Chapter I

THEY GO UP TO POSSESS THE LAND

WHEN John Cooper and Samuel Breeze went riding toward the Redstone Country in the summer of 1784 they must have felt more like explorers than preachers. An impressive scene always marked the close of an early Methodist Conference. Having heard his appointment read, the itinerant immediately located his predecessor. In front of the meeting house where his horse stood in readiness to carry him to his new appointment, he received the plan of the circuit with names of local preachers and class-leaders. A rough map of the route through the wilderness country was sketched, while painstaking care was given to listing homes along the way where hospitality might be extended.

On May 28, 1784, at the Conference in Baltimore, Cooper and Breeze heard their names announced for the Redstone Circuit. Never before had that name appeared in the list of appointments. Redstone signified a destination already famous in border and colonial warfare, but unknown even to Francis Asbury, who at that time probably knew more about American roads than did any other preacher. A new circuit to be carved from lands beyond the Allegheny Mountains held no terrors for John Cooper, who through ten years of itinerating, had already heard his name read out for such distant and perilous frontiers as Tar River, Yadkin, and Cumberland. There was no plan of the Redstone Circuit to be placed in the hands of the two

Methodist pathfinders, for the reason that none existed. It is likely that they sought out Francis Poythress, a far-roving itinerant, who, when on the Alleghany Circuit that extended to the north of the Tuscarawas Mountains, had the previous year penetrated the Redstone Country and had preached in the scattered cabins of the settlers along the Youghiogheny River. This Virginian, who had been signally reclaimed from his youthful waywardness under the preaching of Devereux Jarratt, a Church of England clergyman, had turned from a life of ease to the hardships of frontier preaching before ever he had heard a Methodist preacher. Among all the preachers present at the Baltimore Conference none had an eye quicker to discern spiritual opportunities, or words that would put heart into men face to face with forbidding fields than had Francis Poythress. It may be that Benjamin Roberts, who had accompanied Poythress in raising the standards of Methodism in the ultramontane regions when serving on the Alleghany Circuit, also shared his information with the two recruits assigned to the Redstone Country. James Haw, then fresh in his youthful ardor, who also had made preaching excursions into the regions beyond the Alleghenies, doubtless told the new appointees that they were able to go up and possess the land. He himself in the days before jealousy and contention had dimmed his influence, was able to give a glowing demonstration of what spiritual valor could do in the Indian-infested circuits of Kentucky. If there were others at the Baltimore Conference who should share in the glory of having preceded Cooper and Breeze into their new field of labor, they appear but shadowy figures who wheel their horses and ride off into the silences from the pages of Methodist history.

Having acquired whatever meager information was available, John Cooper and Samuel Breeze rode away from Baltimore for the Redstone Circuit. Like Paul and Barnabas they, as did most early circuit-riders, went two by two in apostolic fashion. Along the Maryland turnpikes, past the manor houses and well cultivated fields, they traveled until they reached the Braddock Road. This they followed along its tortuous windings through Fort Cumberland and over Polish and Big Savage Mountains. They rode onward across Little Meadows below Grantsville and forded the Youghiogheny River at the Great Crossings near Somerfield, Pennsylvania, and ascended Laurel Hill, from which they surveyed the vast and unfamiliar territory which they had been commissioned to transform into a spiritual kingdom.

They little dreamed of the opulence that lay beneath those Pennsylvania hills, but they had an awareness of other riches which they longed to share with the frontiersmen. On the down-trail they passed long pack-trains of horses traveling in single file, laden with gensing, peltries, and produce for the southern markets. And often they fell in with similar caravans conveying salt, rifles, ammunition, and other necessities to the frontier settlements. Already this road which the vanguard of three hundred axemen in 1755 had cleared to a width of twelve feet to create for General Braddock a way over which to lead his troops to the fateful field on the Monongahela, was becoming a highway of commerce. Lured by cheap lands, farmers from Maryland and Virginia were also out on that road in search of what in 1784 was termed "elbow room." Men with rifles across the pommels of their saddles, and women with kneading-boards on their backs and babes in their arms, with destinations no more definite than turned upon the chance of a spot where a grave might be opened up, or their funds exhausted, or an emigrant boat might beach on the Ohio River, were among the riders northward along the Braddock Road one hundred fifty years ago. Jogging along the lonely stretches of this road by day, and sharing the taverns and cabins with the roistering drivers of the pack-trains by night, were John Cooper and Samuel Breeze during the days of early June, 1784.

Doubtless they robbed the journey of some of its monotony by discussing the incidents of the recent Conference. There were the fifteen questions that had been under review and with the answers, tantamount to rules, carefully adopted. "What can be done towards erecting new chapels, and discharging the debts of those already built?" If the former part of the question presented responsibilities they must have chuckled over "discharging the debts" on a circuit that was churchless. "How can we prevent superfluity in dress among our people?" Answer: "Let the preachers carefully avoid everything of this kind among themselves, and speak frequently and faithfully against it in all our societies." Their risibilities must have been further heightened when they looked upon men rigged out in tallowed cowhide boots, linsey-woolens, and buckskin hunting shirts, and women in sunbonnets and drab homespun. And with their own wardrobes consisting of apparel probably plain, patched and shiny enough already on their backs, the problem of preventing "superfluity in dress" on the part of the two preachers was already fully met. "How shall we reform our singing?" At least Brothers Cooper and Breeze had opportunity for self-improvement by raising some of Charles Wesley's tunes as they rode knee to knee through the solitary glades and forests en route to the Redstone Circuit.

In addition to frequent reviews of the deliberations of the Conference, they must also have discussed the men who participated in them. They had listened to Caleb B. Pedicord with his appealing pathos, and to Francis Poythress with his dauntless faith. In debate Nelson Reed had left memories of his convincing logic, and the softening power of divine grace had not completely eradicated the invectives of Joseph Everett when he was aroused. John Dickins, weak of voice, but always convincing because of his orderly mind and businesslike proposals, had commanded their attention, as also had the quips of Peter Moriarity, whose glints of Gaelic wit were always sufficient to enliven the dullest Conference session. Towering above all of them, however, in their memories was Francis Asbury, patient, methodical, commanding, and utterly unsparing in his devotion to Christ and the cause of Methodism.

The reasons for the apparent neglect of Pennsylvania as a field of missionary effort by early Methodism is accounted for with difficulty. By the year 1784 the English missionaries sent out by Mr. Wesley to America had for the most part slipped down from their saddles and taken to the boats, homeward bound, due to the Revolutionary War. Robert Williams, who had arrived in 1769, had confined his ministry largely to Maryland and Virginia, and in 1775 had hunted out a grave near Norfolk, Virginia. Joseph Pilmoor had ranged as far south as Charleston, South Carolina, and Richard Boardman had held to the well-beaten paths at the ends of which lay Boston, New York, Philadelphia, and Baltimore. It is true that Richard Webster, Francis Asbury, Robert Strawbridge, Jesse Lee, and probably others, had preached in the boyhood home of Henry Boehm in Lancaster County, and Benjamin Abbott, did move down the Lancaster Pike in an heroic and breath-taking gospel swing. For the most part York was the most westerly part reached in Pennsylvania, save for some touch-and-go invasions, along the fringe of its southern counties, by Maryland circuit-riders.

The hazards of travel over Pennsylvania roads were certainly no greater than many along the southern frontier over which Methodist preachers had passed for a decade prior to 1784. For twenty years before this commerce had been carried on by pack-horse travel between Philadelphia and the Forks of the Ohio, as Pittsburgh was then called. On the Lancaster-Bedford Road, Fort Lowther had been established in 1753, Fort Chambers at Chambersburg in 1756, Fort Lyttleton at McConnellsburg in 1757, and Fort Bedford in 1751. Forbes Road with Bedford, Ligonier, and Hannastown on its route, had been cut through to Fort Pitt in 1758, and over it the Conestoga wagon, "the vehicle of empire," had jolted for years before Cooper and Breeze arrived on horesback by the back door from the southeast.

Did the anti-Tory feeling in Pennsylvania make the field too forbidding for Methodist preachers who were suspected of British sympathies? It would seem that it could have been scarcely more violent than Asbury found it in Delaware, and Garrettson, Hartley, and Gatch found it in Maryland. Can the fact that the Methodists did not go up to possess the land be attributed to the strength of the numerous defenders of the faith of Martin Luther in Pennsylvania? It must be remembered that it was the country of Bishop Otterbein, Jacob Albright, and Martin Boehm. When George Whitefield met Richard Boardman and Joseph Pilmoor in Philadelphia, he is reported to have informed them in substance that if they would turn Calvinists they would sweep America for Christ. Jesse Lee in New England, and the able controversialists William Burke and Valentine Cook, were to demonstrate conclusively that a doctrinal point, stubborn as it was in that day, could not stop the march of Methodism. Indeed Jesse Lee told Thomas Ware that Methodism could live wherever men could live. What, then, were the reasons why Pennsylvania, as late as 1784, had scarcely been cultivated by Methodists as a missionary field outside the city of Philadelphia and the counties of Bucks, Lancaster, Montgomery, Chester, Berks, and York? Why are there scarcely any records of Methodist itinerants on Pennsylvania roads at a time when they were on almost all other American highways and traces? Not until 1789 did Bishop Asbury make an east-to-west journey across Pennsylvania.

Let us now return to John Cooper and Samuel Breeze, whom we left surveying their extensive parish from the heights of Laurel Hill in 1784. Reference has already been made to certain preachers who were present at the Conference in Baltimore when these two gentlemen received their appointments to the Redstone Circuit. That we may have before us a picture of the quality of the men who composed that valiant brotherhood, we quote from an eyewitness. Thomas Ware, converted under the ministry of Caleb B. Pedicord in New Jersey, and early commandeered by Bishop Asbury for service in the itinerant ranks, has left this impressive description: "Although there were but few on whose heads time had begun to snow, yet several of them appeared to be wayworn and weatherbeaten into premature old age. . . . I doubt whether there has ever been a Conference among us in which an equal number could be found, in proportion to the whole, so dead to the world, and so gifted and enterprising, as were present at the Conference of 1784." [1]

In that company of worthies was John Cooper, a plain, faithful, and effective evangelist. Following his conversion he was discovered kneeling in prayer by his father. So vexed was he at his son's fellowship with the Methodists that he tossed upon him a shovelful of glowing embers. Undaunted by parental persecution he was admitted to the itinerancy, on trial, in 1775, and appointed with Philip Gatch to the Kent Circuit. There, with unflinching courage, he passed through another fiery ordeal in company with Gatch, who had recommended him to the traveling ministry—a series of persecutions scarcely exceeded in the annals of Methodism. Long after his youthful co-laborer in suffering was dead, Philip Gatch paid him a tribute of rare beauty and tenderness. That the measure of devotion and spiritual hardihood of one of the first preachers ever appointed to serve within the bounds of the Pittsburgh

---

[1] Ware, Rev. Thomas, "Sketches of the Life and Travels," written by himself (New York, 1840), p. 83.

Conference may be kept in remembrance, we quote the brief memoir by an unknown writer, printed following his death in 1789: "John Cooper, fifteen years in the work; quiet, inoffensive, and blameless; a son of affliction, subject to dejection, sorrow, and sufferings; often in want, but too modest to complain, till observed and relieved by his friends. He died in peace."[2]

Of the career of Samuel Breeze, the associate of John Cooper on the Redstone Circuit, less is known. His name first appears in 1783 in the appointment to Annamessex Circuit, and in 1793 he is listed under the question, "Who are under a location through weakness of body or family concerns?" In the latter year there was a pronounced restlessness among the preachers due to the agitation for reform led by James O'Kelly. It is possible that this may account in part for the disappearance of the name of Samuel Breeze from the ranks of the Methodist itinerants. During the decade of his ministry he rode some of the most extensive and difficult circuits among which were Annamessex, Redstone, Frederick, Huntingdon, Rockingham, Fairfax, and Alleghany. That he made full proof of his ministry while on the Redstone Circuit is attested to by such a trustworthy witness as James Quinn.

On Thursday, July 1, 1784, Francis Asbury made this entry in his Journal: "We began to ascend the Allegheny, directing our course towards Redstone." At this time he was approaching his fortieth birthday, having been born in Handsworth, Staffordshire, England, August 20, 1745. At the Conference in Bristol, England, August, 1771, he had volunteered

---

[2] Minutes of the Annual Conferences for the years 1773-1839 (New York, 1840), Volume 1, p. 33.

for missionary service in America. After a fifty-three-day voyage he had arrived in Philadelphia on October 27 of the same year in company with Richard Wright. Save for the period between 1778 and 1780 when he was in seclusion in the home of Judge Thomas White in Kent County, Delaware, due to the wave of anti-Tory sentiment then raging against Methodist preachers, he had given himself unsparingly as a missionary. Although he was scarcely past middle age, the years of exposure from incessant travel, the sparse and unpalatable fare of frontier tables, and the fevers contracted from the miasmic swamps of the South, had already made pronounced inroads upon his health.

Following the adjournment of the Conference at Baltimore, Mr. Asbury set out on a tour through Maryland and the present state of West Virginia, with the Redstone Circuit as his objective. There traveled with him Hezekiah Bonham, who in 1772 had ridden with him over the hills of Carroll County, Maryland, on his first visit to the home of Robert Strawbridge. After hearing Bonham preach, perhaps in the Old Log Meeting House on Sam's Creek, Asbury made this entry in his Journal: "I have heard him give an exhortation greatly to the purpose; and gave him a note of recommendation to do all the good he could." The name of Hezekiah Bonham, which first appears in the Minutes of 1785, has found a more enduring place in the membership of the early society on the tablet bearing the legend, "Birthplace of American Methodism," erected at the Robert Strawbridge home by the American Methodist Historical Society.

As they journeyed towards the northwest, Asbury noted in his Journal the effect of the ice jams on the Potomac, "smoothing the river banks as though many hundreds of men had been employed for that purpose." Arriving at "Sister Bodystone's, one of the kindest women in Virginia," he writes, "I was sleepy, weary, and feeble, but my body and soul were refreshed; thanks be to God for every friend!" At Martinsburg he preached to a hundred people. At Stroud's he "spoke with great plainness; the people stared upon us." On Sunday, June 20, he records: "I attempted to preach at Newton. I raged and threatened the people, and was afraid it was spleen." At Strayer's five days later, while kneeling at prayer in a meeting in a grove, a sycamore limb fell into the midst of the worshipers with injury to no one. "Some thought it was a trick of the devil: and so it might have been. Perhaps he wanted to kill another (Bonham?) who spoke after me with great power." He and Bonham filled half a dozen preaching engagements along the way before arriving on July 4 at Cheat River where he writes, "We had a mixed congregation of sinners, Presbyterians, Baptists, and it may be, of saints." "Three thick—on the floor—such is our lodging," was the saint's rest that night.

And so the Lord's emissaries, jaded and feverish under a long drought but recently broken, descended Laurel Hill, rode across the flats and into Beesontown (Uniontown). Of this historic visit to the little frontier village through which the Redstone Creek wound to turn old Henry Beeson's millwheel, Francis Asbury, as if too engaged to write more, has left only these few words: "Pennsylvania—Wednesday, (July) 8. We had nearly seven hundred people at Beeson-Town; they were, in general, serious and attentive." The Field Marshal of Methodism had arrived beyond the Alleghenies.

CHAPTER II

OUTPOSTS OF ZION

THE Redstone Circuit was so named to designate the new work in the Redstone Country. And the Redstone Country was a region of rather indefinite boundaries lying in the valleys drained by Redstone Creek and the Youghiogheny and Monongahela Rivers. It derived its name from Redstone Old Fort, the site of prehistoric Indian earthworks, where Brownsville now stands. As early as 1740 Indian guides led southern traders over these trails to barter with their red tribesmen there. In 1753 Major George Washington passed that way to warn off the French in the name of Governor Dinwiddie. When the Ohio Company was formed in 1748 to wrest the Indian fur trade from the encroaching French, Colonel Jacob Cresap of Old Town, Maryland, engaged as guide the Delaware Indian, Nemacolin, and by 1753 had cut a trader's path through to Redstone Old Fort. On February 17, 1754, Captain Trent, under authority of the Ohio Company, arrived with workmen and began the erection of the "Hangar" at Redstone Old Fort as one of the three storehouses in which to gather commodities for the expected colonists, and merchandise for barter with the Indians on the 500,000 acres which had been acquired by royal grant. Not until Colonel James Burd in 1759, under order of Colonel Henry Boquet, cut through a road and established Fort Burd did commercial activities begin in earnest. The name of Burd faded, but the fame of Redstone was carried to the end of every trader's path and soldier's expedition. "The New Purchase," the title given the lands in this section of Pennsylvania following the council at Fort Stanwix between the Six Nations and the proprietories of the Commonwealth in the autumn of 1768, gave a great impetus to immigration. Yankees from their impoverished hillside farms in New England, Quakers from their eastern settlements, Marylanders and Virginians from the old homesteads to the south, and others with the land-hunger, came, having heard the news, misleading as it proved to be, that in the fertile valleys formerly haunted by savage red men, the white man might take up his abode in safety and peace.

To this vanguard of civilization John Cooper and Samuel Breeze came to minister grace to the hearers. It was a lonely land where the comforts of religion were inadequately offered. It was also the rendezvous of desperate characters whose crimes had made them exiles from their old communities. The Revolutionary War, just concluded, had left the aftermath of a debased moral and spiritual tone such as always follows camp and field. And, as in every frontier environment, there was an inclination to ignore the moral restraints observed in the more orderly surroundings from which many had come.

Long before the outriders of Methodism had alighted from their horses at the cabin doors in the Pennsylvania wilderness, a faithful and effectual witness had been borne by other individuals and denominations. There was Conrad Weiser, who kept the faith in all this region when scalping knives flashed and tomahawks were kept crimson. He was not only the ablest interpreter in the employment of the colonial authorities, but among the savage tribes he walked with true Christian demeanor, even as he vowed he would when, as a novice of the German Seven Day Baptists in their monastery at Ephrata he was consecrated Brother Enoch. In 1748 he went paddling down the Allegheny and Ohio Rivers to Logstown, now Ambridge. For ten days during August he and George Croghan and Andrew Montour were prevented from talking peace with the Indians because of their besotted state. Then the trio began the first temperance crusade recorded in these parts by staving in eight casks of whisky that Henry Noland was vending. The faith and the patriotism of Conrad Weiser were not only transmitted to his daughter, Anna, who married Henry Melchior Muhlenberg, founder of the Lutheran Church in America, but lived again in their children, Frederick A. Muhlenberg, the Lutheran preacher who presided at the Pennsylvania Convention of 1783 that ratified the Constitution, and of John Peter Gabriel Muhlenberg, who in his Woodstock, Virginia, pulpit divested himself of his clerical gown, and in the soldier's uniform beneath, strode down the aisle, swung himself into the saddle, and years later came back from Valley Forge, Monmouth, and points north, a major general.

Then came Charles Christian Post, the plain, uneducated Moravian missionary. If better steel has been produced along the Ohio River than this Christian exhibited in his nerves down at Beaver, then called Sankonk, Pennsylvania, on August 2, 1758, it deserves the prize. There is a legend that George Washington read prayers during the siege of Fort Necessity, and that shortly afterwards Christopher Gist was doing the same for his assembled colonists at Mount Braddock with Indians joining, and with Andrew Montour, the half-breed, acting as interpreter for the latter. In his Journal Colonel James Burd notes that although work was continued on Sunday, time was taken out to hear the chaplain, the Reverend Francis Allison.[1]

In a day when a believer ran the risk of getting a tomahawk in his back if he knelt and shut his eyes to pray, Baptist preachers, who were never inclined to forego salvation for safety, zealous and unafraid, shepherded the sheep in the wilderness. Fourteen years before John Cooper and Samuel Breeze arrived at Uniontown, the Great Bethel Baptist Church had been constituted, and by 1780 plans for the erection of two churches in the community were under way. Among the Baptists, the Redstone Association was the earliest organized west of the Allegheny Mountains. Among its pioneer preachers were John Sutton and John Corbly. Besides those formed near Uniontown, the earliest congregations were at Big Whitely, Greene County, in 1770; Peter's Creek, near Library, Allegheny County, 1773; and at Ursina, in the Turkeyfoot Settlement near Confluence, about the same date.

The Presbyterians claim that "the first minister of the gospel, if we except chaplains of armies, who ever set foot on western soil" was James Finley, who arrived in 1765.[2] The Redstone Presbytery was formed at Pigeon Creek congregation, Washington County, September 19, 1781. As early as September 7, 1766, Charles Beatty preached to the garrison, and Mr. Duffield to the townspeople at

---

[1] Veech, James, "The Monongahela of Old" (Pittsburgh, 1858-1892), p. 32.

[2] For an account of the beginnings of Presbyterianism in southwestern Pennsylvania, see "Old Redstone," by Joseph Smith, D.D. (Philadelphia, 1854).

Fort Pitt. John McMillan made a preaching tour through the region in 1775 which, for daring and hardship, is among the great exploits in the annals of American Protestantism. Perhaps no other minister of western Pennsylvania has ever made so helpful and so extensive a contribution to religion and education as did this eminent pioneer during his labors of almost threescore years in this region. Among the prominent co-laborers of his early days were James Powers, Joseph Smith, Thaddeus Dodd, and James Dunlap. Presbyterian congregations were formed at Dunlaps about 1775; Chartiers, Pigeon Creek, and Mt. Pleasant in 1776; Rehoboth and Lebanon in 1778; and Bethel and Buffalo in 1779.

Perhaps as early as 1770 Lutherans were worshiping in their own meeting house in German Township, and by 1774 had erected a second in Georges Township, both in Fayette County. By September, 1782, Johann Wilhelm Weber, whose parish extended to German settlements over a wide area of southwestern Pennsylvania, had organized a little company of his fellow countrymen into a congregation to be known as the Smithfield Street German Evangelical Church. So closely was the Church of England associated with the British government during the formative years of western Pennsylvania, that the settlers had scant hospitality for its clergymen. That in part accounts for the sparsity of early Protestant Episcopal churches west of the Alleghenies. Various claims for the date of the erection of St. Thomas Church, seven miles northwest of Brownsville, in Washington County, have been made.[8] It is quite certain that

---
[8]See article by Charles W. Dahlinger, Vol. II, p. 69, Western Pennsylvania Historical Magazine.

not later than 1777 it was attended by worshipers who were not infrequently disturbed by alarms of Indian depredations. Not until May 25, 1824, is there record of a visit by a bishop of the Protestant Episcopal Church as far west as Pittsburgh. There are records of other individuals, such as Thomas Hardie, who stood guard over sacred things in a rather unorthodox but effective manner.[4]

This rather extended review of those who manned the outposts of Zion in western Pennsylvania has been given, not only that due recognition might be given the heroes of other communions, but that the reader may have before him a picture of the religious life of the country as it presented itself to the first Methodist itinerants, John Cooper and Samuel Breeze. Of the influences that induced Methodism to extend its metes and bounds to include the Redstone Circuit there are no records available. Some speculations, however, are warranted. In the first place, from his Journals we learn that Francis Asbury for some time had not only been baffled, but impatient with the slow progress of Methodism in the North. Perhaps one of the goads that prodded him on was in the form of statistics. For example, in 1784 there were 13,381 members of his societies south of the Mason and Dixon Line, but only 1,607 north of it. And that line followed the southern boundary of Pennsylvania. Furthermore, the December previous to his arrival in Uniontown, Mr. Asbury had received a letter from Mr. Wesley appointing him general assistant of the work in America. Under the authority and responsibility of that commission he quite naturally felt an obligation to extend the work into

---
[4]For an account of this eccentric preacher, see "Notes on the Settlement and Indian Wars," by Joseph Doddridge (Pittsburgh, 1912), p. 76.

new fields. At the Conference in Baltimore, Mr. Asbury made this entry in his Journal: "William Glendenning has been devising a plan to lay me aside, or at least to abridge my powers; but Mr. Wesley's letter settled that point, and all are happy." There are times when criticism is quite as conducive to extended effort as is a commission. And it may have been a factor in sending the first preachers to the Redstone Circuit.

There were, however, forces more impelling than these. If statistics and criticism may possibly have played a part in sending Francis Asbury across the Allegheny Mountains once, they do not account for the driving power that caused him to scale their heights sixty-two times. The impetus that sent the early circuit riders along all roads and over the rim of every western horizon, was a spiritual yearning to which they always referred in the beautiful expression, "a love of souls." That was the inspiration.

Nor can the arrival of John Cooper and Samuel Breeze on the Redstone Circuit be accounted for without due cognizance of certain local preachers. They first raised the Macedonian call in the great valley of the Ohio. News that a "great door and effectual" had been opened by these local preachers in the Redstone Country, was doubtless carried by Poythress, Haw, and Roberts to the Conference sitting in Baltimore in May, 1784. They constitute an heroic company whose services as heralds of the gospel, as layers of the foundations of the Church, and as moulders of frontier life await just recognition.

Earliest of these in Western Pennsylvania was Reason Pumphrey. The Registry of St. Margaret's

Parish, Church of England, Anne Arundel County, Maryland, 1673-1885, page 54, contains this entry: "Reason Pumphrey, the son of Joseph and Anna Pumphrey, was born the 23rd day of January 1735."[5] Six brothers and two sisters are also mentioned. In 1772, Reason Pumphrey arrived in Washington County, where he settled on a tract of a thousand acres of land at the head of Chartiers Creek. With him came Eli Shickle, also a local preacher who, like Pumphrey, is said to have been converted under the ministry of Robert Strawbridge. While there is a dearth of Methodist local history contemporary with the labors of these two pioneers, it is nevertheless difficult to reconcile the scant attention given them by those who followed in their footsteps and wrote of the beginnings of Methodism, with the posthumous praise given them. Half a dozen men who trace the origin of congregations, name classleaders, exhorters, and other local preachers, leave the name of Pumphrey unmentioned. Even the Journals of Francis Asbury, which abound with the names of preachers and laymen, contain this single reference to Pumphrey who had attended a Quarterly Conference at John Beck's on September 5, 1803: "I came with Rezin Pomfry down the great hill, to the Ohio." When, however, one turns to the histories of local congregations written in later times, one is amazed at the number that owe their beginnings to Reason Pumphrey and Eli Shickle. In large measure this can doubtless be attributed to the fact that instead of devoting their energies to organizing classes and societies, they went about as evangelists content to

---

[5] For this information the author is indebted to Mrs. Arthur Barneveld Bibbins, 2600 Maryland Avenue, Baltimore, Maryland

leave the matter of organization to others that as ambassadors of God they might beseech their hearers on behalf of Christ to be reconciled to God.

When in 1784 John Cooper and Samuel Breeze left Baltimore, their parting instruction had doubtless been that upon their arrival at the foot of Laurel Hill they were to ride straight to the home of Robert Wooster, who lived near Uniontown.* Wooster, who is believed to have arrived in America about the year 1771, had resided in Maryland, where he had come under the quickening influences of the Methodist evangelists, and had migrated to the Redstone Country, where as early as 1781 as a local preacher he was preaching in the settlements of Washington and Westmoreland Counties, before Fayette County had been carved out of the latter. James Quinn, who was reared near Uniontown, says: "He came to one of my appointments in 1799, and preached for me a pure and powerful Gospel sermon. At that time his head and his hair were as white as wool. I felt it a privilege to hear perhaps the first Methodist preacher whose voice was ever heard this side of the Allegheny Mountains."[6] The first recorded Methodist convert in this section appears to have been John Jones, who walked in from his home in Redstone Creek to Uniontown, a distance of ten miles, to hear Robert Wooster, the first Methodist preacher he had ever heard. The manifest interest shown by Jones

---

*In 1777 Robert Wooster had joined the itinerant ministry. Along with Martin Rodda, William Glendenning, and Joseph Cromwell. he was appointed to the Kent Circuit, Maryland. See Minutes of the Annual Conferences, 1773-1828 (New York, 1840), Vol. I, p. 8. In his classification of Methodist preachers from 1769 to the end of 1809 Jesse Lee enters "Robert Worster" in "A List of Methodist Preachers who were only Probationers" under the year 1777. See Jesse Lee, "A Short History of the Methodists" (Baltimore, 1810), p. 339.

[6]Wright, John F., "Sketches of the Life and Labors of James Quinn" (Cincinnati, 1851), p. 34.

caused the old minister to call at the former's home, where during family devotions the seeker was converted. A son of John Jones, Greenbury R. Jones, became an itinerant preacher and rose to a place of prominence in Ohio Methodism. It was he who took into his home two of James Quinn's children when they were left motherless. Robert Wooster, whose godly life left its influence in many frontier communities, moved on with the tide of immigration. About the year 1800 he moved to Bracken County, Kentucky, and later settled near Connersville, Indiana, where he ended his days.

An attempt to recover the names of early local preachers and identify them with localities, leads one into the field of considerable uncertainty. In the vicinity of Uniontown Moses Hopwood, Henry Tomlinson, William McClelland, and perhaps John and Thomas Chaplin, were serving as local preachers as early as 1800. James Quinn worked for John Foot and William Wilson, both local preachers, and from the home of the latter in Fayette County, on June 3, 1799, rode off to his first appointment. Anthony Banning, who was recommended for admission into the itinerancy by the Quarterly Conference of Connellsville about 1789, had been licensed to preach, and local historians claim that down at Brownsville as early as 1776, while the Liberty Bell was proclaiming liberty throughout the land, Chads Chalfant, a local preacher, was hewing the logs for a meeting house. In the neighborhood of Fell's Church, John, eldest son of old Benjamin Fell, and Richard Ferguson were preaching by 1796. It is possible that Henry Shewell, who was converted under the ministry of Ezekiel Cooper, had already received a local preacher's license while at

Waynesburg, Greene County, where he organized a class as early as 1795. Although Thomas McClelland, who had been an itinerant preacher in Ireland, is most usually associated with the section farther north in which he induced Bishop Robert R. Roberts, then a youth, to enter the ministry, the fact that in 1821 he died while en route from Beaver County to Pittsburgh after assisting in meetings in the former locality, leads one to believe that he was occasionally engaged as a local preacher within the present bounds of the Pittsburgh Conference.[7] Gabriel W. and Daniel Woodfield, sons of "The Widow Woodfil" to whom Asbury refers, had migrated to Kentucky from the vicinity of Taylor Church, West Brownsville. Gabriel Woodfield was already a local preacher when he arrived in his Southern home some time before 1800.[8] He played no inconspicuous part in introducing Methodism into Kentucky.

James O'Cull, reared in a Catholic home, and converted to Methodism, was a Redstone Country local preacher fresh from Pennsylvania, when he conducted the funeral service of Samuel Tucker near Limestone, now Maysville, Kentucky. And Samuel Tucker, son of "Father" Tucker, a pioneer Methodist, of Tucker's Station, Washington County, was a local preacher en route to Kentucky as a missionary, when slain by the Indians after bravely protecting the women in a boat at Limestone.[9] It seems probable that Benjamin Lakin, son of the

---

[7] See Methodist Magazine, Vol. 4, pp. 358, 359.

[8] Redford, A. H., "Methodism in Kentucky" (three volumes, Nashville, 1868), Vol. I, pp. 24, 25, 164. Young, Jacob, "Autobiography of a Pioneer" (Cincinnati, 1857), p. 69.

[9] Finley, James B., "Sketches of Western Methodism" (Cincinnati, 1856), p. 44. Redford's "Methodism in Kentucky," Vol. 1, p. 75, and Jacob Young's "Autobiography of a Pioneer," pp. 414-417.

widow, Mrs. Lakin, from near Redstone Old Fort, had been licensed as a local preacher before he migrated to Kentucky with his mother shortly after 1791.[10] Before he left Pennsylvania he had been converted under the preaching of Richard Whatcoat. It was he who received into the Church Dr. John P. Durbin and Bishop Hubbard Hinde Kavanaugh.

In this incomplete review of local preachers we have limited the period to the years prior to 1800, and the field in which they either began, or carried on their labors, to the territory included within the present bounds of the Pittsburgh Conference. Others there were, who also held forth the Word of Life to the frontier families in their lonely and scattered settlements. They were the anonymous members of the daring vanguard who led the assault against the powers of darkness, and smoothed the rugged way for those who should come after them.

---
[10]See Redford's "Methodism in Kentucky," Vol. I, pp. 205-209; Finley's "Sketches of Western Methodism," pp. 178-184; Sprague's "Annals of American Pulpit," p. 268.

CHAPTER III

THEY DELIVERED THE FAITH

FIFTEEN years after John Cooper and Samuel Breeze had passed this way, James Quinn arrived. Forty-six years thereafter, when his memory may have been a bit dimmed by age, he attempted to trace the far-wanderings of the itinerants who had preceded him in 1784.[1] He has set down a dozen localities in four Pennsylvania counties and in one West Virginia county where these men had witnessed out of their glowing experiences. "The first society," he says, "was raised in the vicinity of Uniontown, but at whose house I am not certain. Most probably it was David Jenning's or widow Murphy's." He "next found their footsteps on Youghiogheny near the Broad Ford." They crossed over to Rostraver Township in Westmoreland County, where "Benjamin Fell opened his door, and the Lord opened his heart." "We next find our missionaries passing from the forks of the Youghiogheny over the Monongahela River into Washington County, and directing their course up the River, they raised up the standard on Pike Run. Here they are received by William and Jeremiah Riggs and William How." They proceed to Taylor Church, West Brownsville, where "William and Thomas

---
[1] See John F. Wright's "Life and Labors of James Quinn," pp. 35-42.

Hockins (Hawkins) and Joseph Woodfield became the happy subjects of regenerating grace." Quinn identifies the place thus: "As you pass on the National Road eastward, say five miles west of Brownsville, on the left hand, you see a neat stone chapel, called Taylor's; that stands on the spot where stood the little log hut that, some forty-five or fifty years ago, was called Hockin's Meeting-house, and the second, if not the first, Methodist Meeting-house that ever was reared in the great valley." Further westward, "in the immediate neighborhood of Washington, an open door was set before them by F. Lackey." There, also, "old father Abraham Johnson and his house became obedient to the faith." Accepting the invitation of "Mrs. Hazlet who used to go to that class before there was one in town," Cooper and Breeze held services in Washington. "Next, George Frazier, an old eastern-shore man, near Canonsburg, opened his door and the Word was preached; but I think no society raised." They proceeded to the home of John Doddridge, three miles from West Middletown, Washington County, where they likely met the son, Joseph Doddridge, who was to become an itinerant Methodist preacher, an eminent physician, the most tireless and influential clergyman of the Protestant Episcopal Church west of the Alleghenies, and the author of "Doddridge's Notes," a storehouse of early border history.

Continuing in the footsteps of Cooper and Breeze, Quinn next finds "these devoted and indefatigable servants of Christ, raising the flag of Gospel Liberty on Muddy Creek, where they were received by William Shepherd, George Newland, and others—children of the Church—where a society was raised, and a meeting-house built, called Shepherd's meeting-house. It was a small, log building." They continued across Greene County following the Monongahela to "Whitby (Whitely) and Dunkard Creeks, where they met with a kind reception by David and George Boydston, the Longs and others." We shall resume their missionary travels after they have re-entered Pennsylvania after having met the societies on Crooked Creek, at Martin's Church, and in Morgantown, West Virginia. "They again enter into old Fayette, and bearing down the Monongahela River towards Brownsville they establish a preaching-place at a Mr. Robert's, nearly opposite Muddy Creek, two or three miles from the river. Here also a society was raised, and a meeting-house built, called Robert's Meeting-house." So ended the ministerial labors of John Cooper and Samuel Breeze on the Redstone Circuit, as abridged from the report of James Quinn. These pioneer preachers had set a pace for travel and for extending the Kingdom of Christ beyond the Allegheny Mountains that has remained a worthy pattern for those who have followed them in the region they covered during more than a century and a half of Methodist endeavor.

While these itinerants were going the rounds of their circuit, matters of great consequence to American Methodism were transpiring in England. Affairs of Church as well as State have a strange way of leaping the Atlantic. Just as a rifle shot by one of Colonel George Washington's Virginia troopers on the heights of Laurel Hill in May, 1754, was to echo through the chancellories of the Old World, so thirty years later the decision of an English religious leader was to register throughout every American Methodist preaching place. In a house in Bristol, England, at four o'clock on the morning of

September 1, 1784, candles were aflicker and in the shadowy precincts moved John Wesley, preparing to set apart as Superintendent for America Thomas Coke, and to ordain as elders Richard Whatcoat and Thomas Vasey. Mr. Wesley at eighty-one was still the pioneer who after years of study and hesitation had at last liberated himself from the bondage of ecclesiastical usage and custom, and was daring to take the step that, in the eyes of churchmen such as his brother, Charles, would appear not only unscriptural, but even scandalous. When on Sunday, November 1, 1784, Francis Asbury entered Barratt's Chapel, about a mile from Frederica, Delaware, to attend the fall quarterly meeting, to his amazement Dr. Coke, Richard Whatcoat, and Thomas Vasey were present. There was yet another shock in store for him. He expressed it thus: "Having had no opportunity of conversing with them before public worship, I was greatly surprised to see Brother Whatcoat assist by taking the cup in the administration of the sacrament. I was shocked when first informed of the intention of these my brethren in coming to this country: it may be of God."[2] It was not strange that the sight filled Francis Asbury with misgivings, for had he not been a traveling preacher for twenty years, remaining unordained and never venturing to administer the ordinances? And had not James O'Kelly, Nicholas Snethen, and Robert Strawbridge long proven to be a triple thorn in his flesh with their open defiance of his claim that Methodists should receive the sacraments only at the hands of the clergy of the Anglican Church? Indeed about the most unbrotherly statement to be found in all As-

[2] Asbury's Journal, Vol. I, p. 484.

bury's writings is contained in his comment a few months after Strawbridge's death. On September 3, 1781, he put quill to paper expressing his reflections thus: "Upon the whole, I am inclined to think the Lord took him away in judgment, because he was in a way to do hurt to his cause; and that he saved him in mercy, because from his deathbed conversation he appears to have hope in the end." [3] Before the historic Christmas Conference had adjourned on January 3, 1785, however, Francis Asbury had received ordination as deacon, elder, and General Superintendent at the hands of Dr. Coke, who had received the last-named rite at the hands of Mr. Wesley.

When Bishop Asbury rode away from the Christmas Conference with his newly acquired parchments in his saddlebags, and with news for Methodists along his itinerary that the Conference had acted favorably on the letter of Mr. Wesley in which he recommended ordination for Methodist preachers, a new era was opening for the societies that hitherto had neither denominational status nor sacramental privileges. How urgent was the need for investment of authority in itinerant preachers to administer the ordinances is shown in the entry of Richard Whatcoat's Journal for May 22, 1785. He wrote: "I preached at Wharton, in Kent County, in the morning, and baptized 36 children, and in the afternoon I preached at John Angers, and baptized 50 more." [4]

When the westward hegira began, the type of religion men carried with them bristled with doc-

---

[3] Asbury's Journal, Vol. I, p. 431.

[4] Bradley, Sidney Benjamin. "The Life of Bishop Richard Whatcoat" (Wilmore, 1937), p. 85.

trinalism. As each denomination approached the frontier the more iron-clad became its articles of faith, and the more active and noisy its doctrinal disputants. Not infrequently a leader looked upon a neighborhood in which another communion was dominant as enemy country. The Pauline motto, "Not that we have dominion over your faith, but are helpers of your joy," was not a governing motive as in present-day Protestantism. Modern Presbyterians may be amused at the custom practiced one hundred and fifty years ago in Western Pennsylvania, of "fencing the tables" at a communion service. Then, however, the drastic procedure seemed necessary in order to keep the faith pure. Baptists, likewise, view with wonder the monopoly on salvation which their spiritual forebears maintained they held in the practice of immersion. Methodism was no less intolerant in its sweeping claims of having rediscovered the true apostolic secret of ushering in the kingdom of God.

Be that as it may, Mr. Wesley helped his followers greatly when he penned in Bristol, England, on September 10, 1784, "a little sketch" recommending ordination of his American preachers, and vesting in them the authority to administer the sacraments. In it he also said, "And I have prepared a liturgy, little differing from that of the Church of England, which I advise all the Travelling preachers to use on the Lord's day, in all the congregations, reading the litany only on Wednesdays and Fridays, and praying extempore on all other days." Now it so happened that Western Pennsylvania had in it many Marylanders and Virginians who had been reared in the Church of England. Due to the Revolutionary War the activities of their clergymen had been greatly disrupted because of their suspected sympathy with the British cause, and they had not followed their members who had trekked off to the Pennsylvania frontier. The Presbyterians, who from the first were in the ascendancy in numbers and influence in the Redstone Country, quite generally declined to administer the sacraments to them unless they would subscribe to the Westminster Confession of Faith. Baptists debarred them from communion unless they would renounce their mode of baptism, and receive immersion. To these religious exiles, by the action of the Christmas Conference of 1784, Methodism brought a liturgy with which they were familiar, and a form of sacramental usage almost identical with their own. These facts in large measure explain why the prevailing number of early accessions to Methodism in Western Pennsylvania were from settlers who had been reared in the Church of England back in the old States. And as we review the years ahead we shall discover what an advantage the organization of the Methodist Episcopal Church with an ordained ministry proved to be in the Redstone Country after 1784.

CHAPTER IV

MORE OF THE LORD'S HORSEMEN ARRIVE

LATE in May, 1785, from the heights of Laurel Hill John Cooper and Samuel Breeze took their final view of the field to which they had given such heroic and sacrificial labors. During their sojourn on the Redstone Circuit it could not be charged that "they were not valiant for truth upon the earth." At the Conference which convened in Baltimore on June first, Cooper was appointed to the Little York Circuit and Breeze to the Frederick Circuit. Bishops Coke and Asbury came riding across from Mount Vernon where, on May twenty-sixth, "we waited on General Washington; he received us very politely, and gave us his opinions against slavery," to quote the latter. The two recently ordained General Superintendents had also ridden together through South Carolina in February. Just how congenial they were as riding companions is uncertain, for Bishop Asbury usually rode with one hand on his pulse, while Bishop Coke, with a sweep of the arm, was given to point out the beauties of land and sky.

At the Christmas Conference in Lovely Lane Chapel twelve preachers had received ordination as elders, and each at the Conference of the following June was appointed to administer ecclesiastical matters in one of as many districts. Although the term "presiding elder" was quite inadvertently used as early as 1789, it did not come into general usage until a decade later. Thomas Foster was appointed elder of the region in which the Redstone Circuit was included, with authority to administer the sacraments. Peter Moriarty, John Fidler, and Wilson Lee were appointed to the circuit and were soon scaling the Alleghenies, beyond which lay the vast field in which Cooper and Breeze had pioneered. There is reason to believe that Foster, Moriarty, and Lee had attended the Christmas Conference.[1] In his historic sixteen-hundred-mile ride heralding that assemblage of preachers, Freeborn Garrettson had not reached the fastnesses of Western Pennsylvania to invite Cooper and Breeze.

When Thomas Foster was given supervision of the Redstone Circuit he had been for five years in the itinerant ministry. In 1792 he located on a small farm in Dorchester County, Maryland, where for nearly thirty years he led a most exemplary life, giving unsparingly of his time to every religious effort in that section of the Peninsula. One who knew him long and intimately has written: "No minister was more esteemed on account of sound talent and a holy life than the Rev. Thomas Foster. Mr. Asbury said he was 'of the old stamp, and steady'; and when he was making the circuit of the Peninsula he was pleased to turn in to the pleasant little cottage of Brother Foster, to tarry for a night. Those who were acquainted with him saw a fair specimen of the first race of Methodist preachers."[2]

---

[1] See Lednum, John, "A History of the Rise of Methodism in America" (Philadelphia, 1862), p. 413.

[2] Lednum, John, "History of the Rise of Methodism in America," p. 305.

Peter Moriarty brought to his work on the Redstone Circuit a rugged constitution and orderliness in administration, and, above all, a character singularly attractive because of its saintliness. When he arrived at a preaching place, placed his saddlebags beside the rude pulpit and knelt to pray, the worshipers felt from his reverential attitude that a man of God was preparing to address them. He was born of Catholic parents in Baltimore County, Maryland, April 27, 1758, and until his sixteenth year accepted the training of that Church. His affiliation with the Methodist society in his neighborhood, according to his statement, led his father to look upon him as "a graceless child." Entering the traveling ministry he assisted in the great revivals that were then sweeping through Virginia. Of his appearance near Uniontown, James Quinn says: "Moriarty was the first man I ever heard preach; I was then a lad in my eleventh year. His text was Hebrews 12. 1. Under that sermon I concluded myself a sinner, and that anger was the sin that most easily beset me. Whether this was correct or not, I have profited greatly by it through life thus far. These men were greatly beloved by the people, and very useful among them; and the first generation of Methodists in that region of country loved, and thought, and talked about their beloved Cooper, Breeze, Moriarty, Lee, etc., as long as they lived. Blessed preachers! Blessed people!"[3]

Joseph Crawford, who conducted Moriarty's funeral service, has left a description of this early preacher of the Redstone Circuit in an obituary notice prepared by him. He says: "Although he

---

[3] Wright, John F., "Life and Labors of James Quinn," p. 43. For an account of Moriarity's death, see Spicer, Tobias, Autobiography of (New York, 1852), p. 47.

might not have been classed among the greatest preachers, certainly he was among the most useful; plain in his dress; plain in his manners, and plain and pointed in his preaching, upright in all his deportment; in short, his life was a constant comment upon the gospel he preached."[4] He had been among the young men who responded to the call of Freeborn Garrettson to extend the boundaries of Methodism along the Hudson River. At the time of his death, which occurred suddenly at Hillsdale, New York, June 23, 1814, he was a Presiding Elder of the New York Conference. One sees an indication of the driving energy of this evangelist in the complaint of John Lee, already ill, who felt that, due to the exposure to inclement weather exacted of him by Moriarty in riding the New Rochelle Circuit in 1789, he had undermined his health.[5]

John Fidler served the Redstone Circuit in 1785, and after his appointment to the Fairfax Circuit the next year, his name disappears like those of the lost kings of Judah. There is reason to believe that he was a native of New Jersey. Because of his brief period of three years in the itinerancy, the facts of his ministry are rather meager.

When Wilson Lee arrived with his associates on the Redstone Circuit he was but twenty-four years of age, and had just been received on trial into the itinerant ministry at the recent Conference. Few men in Methodism have left a memory so fragrant, and a name so blameless as has Wilson Lee. With the passing of the years a great silence has fallen over the places that were blessed with his ministry

---

[4]Minutes of the Annual Conferences, 1773-1828, Vol. I, p. 241.

[5]See Lee, Jesse, "A Short Account of the Life and Death of the Rev. John Lee" (Baltimore, 1805), p. 76.

in this region. Across the years, however, have come countless testimonies to his polished manners, his distinguished appearance, his well-trained and pleasant voice, his humility, and, above all, to the effectiveness of his preaching, which was "with the demonstration of the spirit and with power." Young though he was, along whatever road Wilson Lee moved he brought the comfort and the hope of the gospel to the cabin-dwellers of the Pennsylvania frontier. Reared in a home of refinement in Delaware, and possessed of exceptional advantages, he matched his talents and his body, always rather frail, against the deprivations and the dangers of the farthest extremities of civilization that he might win some for Christ.

After leaving the Redstone Circuit he was appointed to Kentucky, where through seven years he often suffered hunger, was in péril of savages, and at times spent a night lost in the wilderness. Henry Smith, who shared his sufferings in that State in an early day, in recalling those who there laid the foundations of Protestantism, says, "Among them was Wilson Lee, who went through that country like a blazing torch; the rich as well as the poor followed him, 'and much people was added to the Lord.' "[6] Although in no sense a backwoods preacher of the type of Peter Cartwright, he would have continued his services along the frontier had his health been sufficient to endure its hardships. With that ease of adaptability that characterizes the gentleman wherever found, but with no surrender of his spiritual fervor, Mr. Lee entered upon pastorates in New York City and St. George's Church, Philadelphia,

---

[6] Smith, Henry, "Recollections and Reflections of an Old Itinerant" (New York, 1848), p. 49.

and closed his brief but enviable ministerial career as a Presiding Elder of the Baltimore Conference.

Nearly a score of years after the intrepid young preacher, Wilson Lee, first rode into the Redstone Country over the Braddock Road, Bishop Asbury was leaving by that same route. Leaving Washington, Pennsylvania, he had stopped at Joseph Taylor's near Taylor's Church, passed through Uniontown, over the Great Crossings, and on to Jacob Cresap's at Old Town, Maryland. It was late October. The Bishop observed the soft haze that hung over the Pennsylvania hills and the warmth and silence that pervaded the valleys. "We have Indian summer," mused the Bishop. And after the resurgence of strength to his own exhausted body, in response to a month's nursing at the home of Harry Stevens, he may have felt that to his own life, which was growing a bit wintry, a spell of Indian summer also had come. He observed this, also: "It is wonderful to see how Braddock's Road is crowded with wagons and pack-horses carrying families and their household stuff westward—to the new State of Ohio, no doubt." Twenty years effected great changes on the frontier. A rumor of the death of Wilson Lee, who had died October 11, 1804, reached Bishop Asbury as he was moving along the Braddock Road. As the Bishop saw the wagons rolling westward along a highway that had been but a pack-trail when first he sent Wilson Lee over it a score of years before, and as he envisioned the flight of loneliness and danger—plenty of which Lee had known—before the advancing population, doubtless his thoughts were occupied with his fallen helper. At Joseph Cresap's, where he spent the Sabbath, he wrote in his Journal: "I saw the death of Wilson

Lee confirmed in the Frederick *Gazette;* he died at Walter Worthington's, in Anne Arundel County, Maryland. Wilson Lee was born near Lewistown, Delaware; he was of a slender habit of body, but active, diligent, and upright in his walk; a pattern of neatness in his habits and attire; and full of gentleness, meekness, and love; his presence commanded respect; his zeal for God was great, and his labours successful, and continually so."[7] In Mount Olivet Cemetery, Baltimore, where so many of the Lord's challengers of far horizons have exchanged the companionship of the road for that of a final halting place for their bodies, Wilson Lee and Bishop Asbury have fittingly sought shelter for the night.

While in 1785 the Redstone Circuit was under the care of spiritual shepherds such as Thomas Foster, elder, and Peter Moriarty, John Fidler, and Wilson Lee, the flock of Christ in the wilderness must have been well fed. During July of that year Bishop Asbury came north through Cumberland and Morgantown and arrived at Uniontown on the nineteenth with a badly inflamed throat and a high temperature. His Journal of that date contains no further account of his visit to Western Pennsylvania than the line "Rode to Litton's, but could not preach. Came on to Beason-Town; gave an exhortation, and rode on to ———."[8]

It seems likely that Bishop Asbury did not meet his preachers on the Redstone Circuit until the Annual Conference convened at Abingdon, Maryland, on May 8, 1786. Cokesbury College had recently been established at this place, which gave its

---
[7] Asbury's Journal, Vol. III, p. 166.
[8] Asbury's Journal, Vol. I, p. 498.

promoters unusual opportunity to exhibit it to the ministers, and incidentally, of course, to enroll them as solicitors to help pay its debt. "Love, candour, and precision marked our deliberations," was Bishop Asbury's estimate of the Conference. It appears, however, that they did not exhibit the same precision about selecting strong men for the Redstone Circuit that had been shown at the preceding session—a variableness of which complaint is still occasionally heard. Enoch Matson, the Presiding Elder, was a preacher with gifts above the ordinary, but for reasons which are unknown he was disowned by the Conference of 1788. It was he who baptized the five children of Mr. and Mrs. John Quinn, of Fayette County, among whom was James, afterward prominent in Methodism. Less gifted perhaps, but held in high esteem for his long and honorable service was John Smith, preacher in charge of the Redstone Circuit. He hailed from Kent County, Maryland, where he was born in 1758. He is described as "a man of slender and delicate constitution." For a decade after he left the Redstone Circuit he served difficult circuits with patience and fidelity. When he died in 1812 he had been for many years on the superannuated list, due to invalidism. Robert Ayres was for four years in the Methodist itinerant ranks, from which he asked to be dismissed in 1789 that he might receive ordination in the Protestant Episcopal Church. The year after Stephen Deakins left the Redstone Circuit his name disappears from the Conference Minutes.

During the year 1786, as usual, Bishop Asbury was exerting every effort to keep the frontier manned with workers, despite the fact that occasionally one disappointed him. "I preached three times, and made a collection to defray the expense of sending missionaries to the western settlements," is his description of how he spent an April Sunday in Baltimore that year. By mid-June he had written in his Journal, "Sick or lame, I must try for Redstone tomorrow." By June twentieth he was in Uniontown hobbling about on a swollen foot. He notes, "Being court time at Besontown, our congregation was large; perhaps not less than six hundred people." [9] Two days later, while crossing the Monongahela at Redstone Old Fort he observed that they were building a town.* The day was made enjoyable by meeting old acquaintances from Maryland. On June 23 he "had many to hear at S. Littons." As he was entering upon a tour of Washington County he observed, "We are now going to the frontiers, and may take a peep into the Indian land." He found the congregation "very still and lifeless at Lackey's" near Washington. Of Sunday, July 25, he writes: "We had a wild company at D————'s. . . . After preaching we ate a little bread and butter, and rode fifteen miles to Doddridge's Fort.† John Smith, the preacher, and other Marylanders arrived to cheer him up. On the morrow he "preached in Coxe's Fort on the Ohio River."‡ In retracing their steps over the fifteen mile route the Bishop and his party became lost, and made the journey in a drenching rain. The next day, Tues-

---

[9] For account of the two weeks spent in western Pennsylvania at this time, see Asbury's Journal, Vol. I, pp. 513, 514.

*Brownsville had been laid out in lots in 1785.

†Doddridge's Fort stood about three miles west of West Middletown, Washington County, Pa. See "Frontier Forts of Pennsylvania," by George Dallas Albert (Charles M. Bush, State Printer of Pennsylvania, 1896), p. 423.

‡The Cox's Fort to which reference is made stood a few miles above Wheeling, West Virginia. See "Frontier Forts of Pennsylvania," Albert, Vol. II, p. 433.

day, June 27, he "had large congregation, and Divine aid," and "hasted away to a little town called Washington—wicked enough at all times, but especially now at court time." On Thursday he "had enlargement in speaking to three or four hundred people at Robert's Chapel." The next day the Bishop "came to the widow Murphy's" near Uniontown, and July first and second "spoke in the new church" in that place, and administered the sacrament. The next day he was in the saddle riding towards Maryland.

When the preachers of the Redstone Circuit arrived at Baltimore from their wilderness parish on May 1, 1787, they witnessed one of the liveliest Conference sessions ever held in the history of Methodism. Because, as that body charged, Bishop Coke had acted arbitrarily in changing the time and place of the Conference that he might attend before sailing for England, he was required to sign a statement that he would not exercise any authority over Methodism while absent from the country, along with a list of official privileges which he would not exceed while in America. The Conference rescinded its agreement, made by formal resolution in 1784, with Mr. Wesley "in matters belonging to Church government, to obey his commands." Of this cutting of the apron strings from the mother Church, Bishop Neely says, "The action was an ecclesiastical Declaration of Independence."[10] In its recalcitrant mood it declined to follow Mr. Wesley's recommendation of making Richard Whatcoat and Freeborn Garrettson General Superintendents unless, in the case of the latter, he would confine his authority to

---

[10] Neely, Thomas B., "The Governing Conference in Methodism" (Cincinnati, New York), 1893, p. 291.

MORE OF THE LORD'S HORSEMEN ARRIVE 53

Nova Scotia. During the heated debate over the episcopal fitness of Richard Whatcoat, and the dropping of Mr. Wesley's name from the Discipline, and of later expunging the minute, Bishop Asbury remained mute, only to find that he was later criticized by both factions. In the outcome of one item of procedure, however, he must have been active, and highly pleased. In response to Question 21, "Where and when shall the Conferences be held next year?" the fifth reply listed was, "At Union Town, on Tuesday, the 22nd of July."

At the Conference of 1787 Joseph Cromwell was appointed elder of the territory that embraced Western Pennsylvania, and William Phoebus, Elisha Phelps, and James Wilson were appointed to the Redstone Circuit. Joseph Cromwell, out of a genuine sympathy by his brethren, received little comment from those who chronicled the events of latter days. His friends preferred to recall only his earlier years when, in the zeal of sharing his newly-found joy, he stirred congregations with unusual power. Thomas Ware, a bit puzzled to understand the success of some preachers who were scholastically limited, cited "Joseph Cromwell, who, though he could not write his name, preached in the demonstration of the Spirit and with an authority that few could withstand. By his labors, thousands, of all classes and conditions in society, had been brought into the fold, and were walking worthy of their profession."[11] How high he stood in the estimation of Bishop Asbury in 1780 is expressed by him in these words: "I thought it would be well for me to have a person with me always, and I think Cromwell is the man. If I should preach a systematical,

---
[11] "Sketches of the Life and Travels of Thomas Ware," p. 94.

dry sermon, he would pay the sinners off." [12] Fourteen years later, with a pathos seldom reached by the Bishop, he wrote of the tragic fall and death of him whose labors and faithfulness he had often recorded in his Journals. His career stands as an illustration of the warning expressed by Paul, lest, "After that I had preached to others, I myself should be a castaway." *

One of the most versatile preachers that ever represented Methodism in Western Pennsylvania was William Phoebus. He was eccentric, independent, and outspoken to a degree that at times threatened his usefulness. In his nature was a rich vein of originality that set him apart from other men. In a day when people followed their favorite preacher from church to church, a large congregation had assembled to hear a celebrated minister only to discover, to their disappointment, that Dr. Phoebus was in the pulpit. During the singing of the first hymn, as they began to leave, Dr. Phoebus called for silence, announced that he shared their views about his preaching, and that if they would wait a minute he would get his hat and go with them.[13]

In spite of his flashing humor he never failed to bring to sacred matters an impressive solemnity and reverence. Born in Maryland in 1754, he witnessed the rise of Methodism in that State, was present at the Christmas Conference, and was early an intimate associate of the founders. At times he

---

[12] Asbury's Journals, Vol. I, p. 393.

*In a volume of the Minutes of the Annual Conferences in the possession of the author there appears a footnote to the notice of Mr. Cromwell's expulsion written in pencil by one whose script indicates that he was very aged. The charitable note reads: "Jos. Cromwell, a reformed drunkard, while sick at Josias Dallam's, was persuaded to take brandy as a medicine contrary to his own wishes and judgment. The fatal appetite was revived. He relapsed into intemperance and so died."

[13] See Wakeley, Rev. J. B., "Lost Chapters Recovered from the Early History of Methodism" (New York, 1858), p. 328.

turned from the ministry to teach, to practice medicine, and to edit a magazine. Yet from his first love, the Church, he never departed. He assisted at the ordination of Bishop Roberts, whom he may have seen, a ten-year-old lad in his cabin home near Ligonier in 1787. He wrote a life of Bishop Whatcoat, and with the love of an antiquarian rescued and preserved in literary form a rich store of Methodist anecdotes and lore concerning those who belonged to that heroic age. When in 1831 he died in New York City, the former rider of the Redstone Circuit had left not a few monuments of enduring worth. He had introduced Methodism into Brooklyn and had laid the cornerstone of the Sands Street Church. He had served on the "Committee of Fourteen to devise and report a plan for a delegated General Conference." In that body he had twice represented the New York Conference. And his acts of devotion, laconic utterances, and long and distinguished service in many fields caused him to be remembered affectionately by a host of friends.

Elisha Phelps came to the Redstone Circuit in 1787 as the associate of William Phoebus and James Wilson. From such accounts as are available he appears to have been a man of rather exceptional attainments. Later he married the widow of Major Hughes of General Braddock's ill-fated command, and retired from the itinerancy to the estate of his father-in-law in Virginia. In 1802 James Quinn was appointed to the Winchester Circuit, and while there he spent a day in the home of Mr. and Mrs. Phelps, and has left a record of the happy fellowship of the ministers of those distant days.[14] He describes how, on August 24, "at an early hour,

---
[14] See Wright's "Life and Labors of James Quinn," pp. 67-74.

before the heat of the day came on, a most interesting company convened at the lovely residence, where true Virginia hospitality, in old style, stood ready to receive them with smiling welcome." Upon the arrival of Bishop Asbury from Winchester, "in order that all things might be sanctified by the word of God and prayer," he was asked to address the throne of grace. Of the host and hostess, Mr. Phelps and his wife, he says: "He had been a traveling preacher of respectable talents. His heart was still warm in the cause, though he had retired from the work. His open, good-natured countenance told his guests that they were welcome, and that was enough. His deeply pious lady, somewhat in advance of him in years, was of olden style, a sensible, well-informed woman. She was a daughter of Colonel Hyte of Revolutionary fame.* Her orderly movements and countenance beaming with good nature said to her friends, Feel yourselves at home." Mr. Quinn presents all the guests to his readers in a most engaging style. The day passed "in a free flow of conversation on a variety of topics, chiefly of a moral and religious character." "Dr. William McDowell, late of Chilocothe, at that time in the prime of life, a man of most dignified appearance: his raven locks, hanging in ringlets, were beginning to be sprinkled with gray; and the fine Irish bloom was yet glowing on his cheek"—it was he who took the lead in the "heart-warming, soul-animating" hymn singing. Forty years thereafter, Mr. Quinn recalled how for grace before meat "the Bishop tuned his musical powers—a deep-toned, yet mellow bass," and how at time of parting they united their

---
*This was Colonel John Hite, early colonizer of the Shenandoah Valley, who obtained a tract of 94,000 acres of land near Winchester, Virginia. See West Virginia Historical Magazine, Vol. III, p. 109.

"musical powers in one of the songs of Zion," and bowed in prayer as the venerable Bishop commended them to the God of peace. Thus has been preserved for us a picture of the later home of one of Western Pennsylvania's early circuit-riders.

James Wilson, who entered upon his apprenticeship in the ranks of the traveling ministry on the Redstone Circuit in 1787, was born on the Eastern shore of Maryland, that recruiting ground of so many other itinerants. Under the rigors of six years of exposure his health failed and he died at Churchill, Queen Anne's County, Maryland, in October, 1793.

It is noteworthy that as the year's work drew to its close the messengers of Methodism in Western Pennsylvania, for the first time, were not obliged to turn towards Baltimore to receive their annual appointments. In four years eleven preachers had ridden up the Braddock Road. Under the supervision of three Presiding Elders, the devoted oversight of Francis Asbury, and the blessing of God they had sown the Word beside all waters, and so promising was the harvest that Methodism had decided to direct its workers from a base on the field.

Chapter V

ALL ROADS LEAD FROM UNIONTOWN

ON July 22, 1788, Bishop Asbury arrived at Uniontown, Pennsylvania, to preside over the second Conference held west of the Allegheny Mountains.* With him traveled Richard Whatcoat, and from the Bishop's account of his having had "to answer many questions propounded to him" near Clarksburg, and later of being obliged to "take to the woods" because of certain inhospitable features at a lodging—rather thoughtless treatment of a crippled preacher—we know that William Phoebus was in the company. Of this first Conference in all this vast region Bishop Asbury makes this brief comment: "Our Conference began at Union Town. We felt great peace whilst together; and our counsels were marked by love and prudence. We had seven members of Conference and five probationers. I preached on 1 Peter 5. 7: and Brother Whatcoat gave us an excellent discourse on "O! man of God, flee these things." [1]

---

*The claim that this was the first Conference held west of the Allegheny Mountains is valid if one accepts the local terminology of the Appalachian Range. If, however, consideration is given to the great barrier that so long prevented migration to the western waters, which we regard as more warranted, then the claim for priority must be conceded to the Conference held at Half-Acres, Tennessee, in May, 1788. Bishop Asbury referred to this range as "the Allegheny Mountains," and if stay-at-homes question his powers of accurate description, they may refer to his Journal (Volume II, p. 31) in which he states: "After getting our horses shod we made a move for Holstein, and entered upon the mountains; the first of which I called steel, the second stone, and the third iron mountain."

[1] Asbury's Journal, Vol. II, p. 38.

Bishop Asbury had not visited the Redstone Circuit for fourteen months. With his arrival at Uniontown he had completed the most memorable visitation of his career, a journey which in its extent and service might fittingly be termed his "grand tour." His traveling companion was Richard Whatcoat who, as we have seen, had been ordained an elder by Mr. Wesley in Bristol in September, 1784, and had arrived in America the following month in company with Dr. Coke. Like Barnabas he was "a good man, full of faith and the Holy Spirit." At the Uniontown Conference he was fifty years of age, had already impressed the Church with his singleness of purpose and with a quality of character referred to as saintliness by his contemporaries. With Christian magnanimity he had, in 1787, accepted the refusal of his brethren to elect him a General Superintendent at Baltimore, as proposed by Mr. Wesley, and pressed on with never a trace of regret or displeasure until that honor was conferred upon him in 1800.

Again we must turn for a description of the Conference at Uniontown to the pioneer preacher, James Quinn, who was the eyewitness of Methodist history in the making in Western Pennsylvania. He gives this account: "I was at that Conference, a lad, in my thirteenth year, and witnessed, I think, the first ordination that ever took place in the great valley. Mr. Asbury officiated, not in the costume of the 'lawn-robed prelate,' but as the plain presbyter, in gown and band, assisted by Richard Whatcoat, the elder, in the same habit. The person ordained was Michael Lord, of whom it was said that he could repeat the whole of the New Testament off the book and large portions of the Old.† The scenes of that day looked well in the eyes of the Church people; for not only did the preachers appear in sacerdotal robes, but the morning service was read, as abridged by Mr. Wesley. But the priestly robes and prayer-book were soon laid aside at the same time; for I never saw the one or heard the other, since."[2]

It was in this same clerical attire mentioned above that Bishop Asbury had appeared at a service in the home of Colonel Hendron, the February following his ordination as General Superintendent that so upset Jesse Lee.[3] If Francis Asbury and Richard Whatcoat alarmed their brethren lest they were going "High Church," their fears were quite unfounded, for on September 20, 1788, two months after the Conference at Uniontown, a fussy little Englishman, aged eighty-five, sat down and wrote a letter in which he took his erstwhile General Superintendent to task for allowing himself to be addressed "Bishop." Apparently the letter did not change the title, but it may have had something to do with removing the gowns.

Of the dozen preachers who attended the Conference in Uniontown in 1788, besides Bishop Asbury and Richard Whatcoat, we are certain of the names of but three — William Phoebus, Michael Leard, and Joseph Doddridge. Dr. Thomas Scott states that Doddridge rode away from Uniontown

---

†The Michael Lord to whom Quinn refers appears in the Minutes as Michael Leard. Mrs. Arthur Barneveld Bibbins thinks that he was Michael Laird, son of an early class leader in Drumsna, Ireland, and that he followed his father's friend, Robert Strawbridge, to Maryland, where he entered the itinerancy. She adds: "After some years he located in Philadelphia, where he lived a useful life and corresponded with Dr. George M. Roberts, founder of the American Methodist Historical Society." Quinn says: "He died in poverty, obscurity, and peace on Cheat River, about forty-one or forty-two years ago" (1840?).

[2]Wright, John F., "Life and Labors of James Quinn," p. 51.

[3]See Thrift, Minton, "Memoir of the Rev. Jesse Lee, with Extracts from his Journals" (New York, 1823), p. 71.

en route to the Holston Circuit with Bishop Asbury.[4] It is highly probable that Joseph Cromwell, the Presiding Elder, and the associates of Phoebus on the Redstone Circuit, Elisha Phelps and James Wilson, were also present. Because of their proximity to, and inclusion in, the district of Cromwell, it is likely that Robert Cann and Richard Pearson of the Clarksburg Circuit, and Charles Conaway and George Callahan of the Ohio Circuit attended. Of but one place does Bishop Asbury make mention during his Pennsylvania visit and that is Doddridge's, Independence Township, Washington County, where he reports "a melting time."

Upon the adjournment of the three-day Conference, Charles Conaway rode off to the newly created Pittsburgh Circuit. He had been received on trial, and gave ten years to the Methodist ministry, seven of which were spent in connection with the Pittsburgh Circuit, two as preacher in charge, and five as Presiding Elder. Perhaps the best description of Conaway and account of his entrance upon his work in Pittsburgh has been given by Dr. W. B. Watkins. He says: "He enters the town by the old Fourth Street Road, ascends the eastern slope of Grant's Hill, and in descending makes a detour to avoid the southern extremity of one of the largest ponds of the village. The man is Charles Conaway, the founder of Methodism in Pittsburgh, who comes now at the behest of the Baltimore Conference and Bishop Asbury, as the first appointed preacher to plant the seeds of the Kingdom in this unpropitious soil. As he pauses, perhaps, to inquire concerning his stopping place, let us scrutinize him more closely, for he, notwithstanding a century of neglect, and

---

[4]Doddridge, Joseph, "Notes on the Settlement and Indian Wars," p. 245.

the fact that mightier footsteps followed close after him, is the central figure of this hour. As he sits there upon his well-conditioned horse, you perceive a medium-sized, compactly-built man of thirty-eight years of age, whose dark hair falls almost to the sturdily rounded shoulders, which make up his contour. You look into his sharp, bluish-gray eyes, and in their far depths may read the story of his devotion. You hear, perhaps, the ring of a voice whose vibratory power is capable of projecting itself to far distances, and whose persuasive accents fell on human hearts with a potent spell."

"This man," continues Dr. Watkins, "before he had enlisted beneath the Cross, had been a soldier of the Revolution, and had served in the struggle for American liberty. Although born on the Eastern Shore of Maryland, he had been a pronounced Abolitionist long before Garrison and Phillips were born. ... This manly man died in Ohio in 1847 ... and his grave in Harrison County, to our shame be it said, is unmarked by fitting memorial to this day."[5]

Almost invariably those who have written of the early denominational missionary efforts in Western Pennsylvania, have pointed out the tardiness with which work was begun in Pittsburgh. The foundations were first laid in rural communities among the yeomanry of sturdier faith than that offered by the traders, freighters, soldiers, and river-men of Pittsburgh. As early as 1761 James Kennedy, a Quaker Indian trader, jotted down in his journal this rather complimentary observation of the spiritual aspirations of early Pittsburghers, "Ye soberer sort of people seem to long for some way of public wor-

---

[5] "One Hundred Years of Pittsburgh Methodism" (Pittsburgh, 1888), pp. 104, 105.

ALL ROADS LEAD FROM UNIONTOWN 63

ship." A score of years and more had passed when Arthur Lee, under date of December 24, 1784, scribbled in his line-a-day this account of their unrealized longings, "There are in the town four attorneys, two doctors, and not a priest of any persuasion—no church, no chapel.[6] When, however, Conaway arrived in Pittsburgh the Presbyterians were worshiping in a log meeting-house on the corner of Wood Street and Sixth Avenue, and an organization with occasional preaching, to which we have earlier referred, had been effected by some German families, the outgrowth of which has become the German Evangelical Protestant Church on Smithfield Street.

The place where Charles Conaway preached, and the names of those who constituted his small congregation have been carried into oblivion by the passing years. Aside from the worshipers who gathered to hear Wilson Lee, according to Dr. F. S. DeHass, "in a tavern which stood on Water Street, near Ferry Street" in the autumn of 1785, there were few to extend a welcome to Pittsburgh's first Methodist preacher. At this date it is impossible to trace with any degree of certainty the boundaries of either the Pittsburgh or Redstone Circuits, and one is left as a means of determining the territory of each only the occasional references to the ministers at certain preaching places.

At the Conference in Uniontown in 1788, from which Charles Conaway rode off to the Pittsburgh Circuit, Jacob Lurton and Lasley Matthews were appointed to the Redstone Circuit with Richard Whatcoat as Presiding Elder. Wherever one comes

---
[6]Thurston, George H., "Allegheny County's Hundred Years" (Pittsburgh, 1888), p. 21.

upon a trace of Jacob Lurton he finds him in the path of righteousness, moving always with the restlessness of a pioneer across many states, and around many circuits. To him belongs that immortality of influence which arises from enlisting others in the Christian ministry. While on the Redstone Circuit in 1788, Lurton was instrumental in the conversion of a lad of fifteen, Samuel Parker, who lived near Uniontown.[7] Few Methodist preachers following the turn of the nineteenth century performed more heroic and sacrificial labors than did Samuel Parker. At his funeral service in Washington, Mississippi, in 1821, those present heard William Winans, another Fayette County boy who attained eminence, tell how Samuel Parker, the sweet singer of Israel, had led him into the Christian way of life. And the far-reaching influences which these two men exerted had their origin in Jacob Lurton. Deep in the forests of Logan County, Kentucky, where he was laboring not far from Gabriel Woodfield, a product of Old Taylor Church, a boy of nine was sent to the homes of the settlers to invite them to hear a circuit-rider in his father's cabin. The preacher was Jacob Lurton, and the lad was Peter Cartwright. On that occasion began the spiritual awakening of the famous backwoods preacher.[8] Lurton moved to Illinois in 1820 where with pride, and doubtless much amusement, he received tidings of the labors of his eccentric Kentucky convert on those frontier prairies. His fruitful life came to a close on the Piasa River near Alton.

Associated with Jacob Lurton on the Redstone Circuit in 1788 was Lasley Matthews. He was an

[7]See Finley, James B., "Sketches of Western Methodism," pp. 202-214.
[8]Cartwright, Peter, Autobiography of (New York, 1858), pp. 23, 24.

Irish Catholic youth who, during the campaigns of the Revolutionary War, shared the tent of a young Frenchman, Joseph Cheuvront, who, in his native land, had been trained for the priesthood. As the latter read from his pocket Bible there began those strange searchings for fuller truth. Eventually both entered the ministry, Cheuvront to become the founder of Methodism in the vicinity of Clarksburg, West Virginia, and Matthews to give twenty-seven years to circuit preaching.[9] On March 24, 1813, Matthews arrived at the home of Isaac Robbins en route to the Baltimore Conference so exhausted that he had to be lifted from his horse by two men and carried into the house. Following his death a few days later, Mr. Robbins wrote a letter to Bishop Asbury which contained this information, "He has left a will, desiring that his horse, saddle, bridle, saddlebags, cloak, greatcoat, and his wearing apparel be sold after his death, and the net amount paid to the treasurer of the Charter Fund."[10]

Since the General Minutes of 1787 list the Clarksburg and the Ohio Circuits it seems erroneous to claim that at the first Conference at Uniontown the Redstone Circuit was divided into four circuits. The records show that the Pittsburgh Circuit alone was formed, but no account of the new alignment that was possibly necessary, is available. In that day of open territory the area of a circuit was quite variable. It is true, however, that in the year 1788 there began that process of dissection and diminution, through giving its life for others, which in 1915 led the Redstone Circuit to "wink out," as Abraham Lin-

---

[9]See Smith, Henry, "Recollections and Reflections of an Old Itinerant," pp. 20, 21.

[10]General Minutes, 1773-1828, Vol. I, p. 224.

coln said of his store. It seems probable from later records that the Ohio Circuit included the county seat towns of Beaver and Washington in Pennsylvania, and the open spaces to the west. Richard Pearson and John Todd, who were admitted on trial in 1787, were appointed to that circuit in 1788, and located two years later.

At this time it may be well to review the trail blazed by the pathfinders, John Cooper and Samuel Breeze, in 1784, as set forth by James Quinn. It will be recalled that, beginning at Uniontown, they established a congregation at Connellsville, visited the society in the neighborhood of Benjamin Fell's three miles west of West Newton, continued down the Youghiogheny, and began the ascent of the Monongahela River near McKeesport. They established work on Pike's Run, moved on to Brownsville, and visiting the society in the community where Taylor Church now stands between Brownsville and Centerville, they turned west to Washington, with a prospecting trip to Canonsburg. They established a preaching place at Doddridge's Fort near West Middletown, Washington County, and then turned southward, following the Monongahela through Greene County to the mouth of the Cheat River. They returned from West Virginia, entering Pennsylvania on the east side of the Monongahela and established a preaching place opposite the mouth of Muddy Creek at a Mr. Robert's. It is important to note, that save for the excursion into Washington County, Cooper and Breeze had confined the field of their labors in Pennsylvania almost exclusively to the settlements along the Youghiogheny and Monongahela Rivers.

That was James Quinn's conception of the extent

of the Redstone Circuit in 1784. He also has left an account of how in 1788 Jacob Lurton and Lasley Matthews extended the borders of that circuit.[11] Their missionary activities began by entering the mountains fifteen miles south of Uniontown. They preached in the communities of the present towns of Somerfield and Confluence. Leaving these they moved through Somerset County to the neighborhood of Berlin where Michael King, an old local preacher, previous to his death that year, had paved the way. Into the membership of the society came D. Moore and the parents of the Reverend John Solomon. Lurton and Matthews then crossed the mountains into the Ligonier Valley where A. McLean and Enos King, son of the old local preacher, offered their homes as meeting places. Near Ligonier "the father of the venerable Bishop Roberts, and his extensive family, although Church people, fell into the ranks of Methodism." Quinn, who wrote his reminiscences more than forty years after he had ridden the Redstone Circuit, must have been confused in his location when he states, "Here, also, was the devout Cornelius Riley (Reiley) and his excellent wife, Abigail, and mother of James and Tobias Riley of the Baltimore Conference."*

Pushing northward the two circuit-riders crossed the Conemaugh River into Indiana County, where they received hospitable welcome in the home of

---

[11]See Wright, John F., "Life and Labors of James Quinn," pp. 52-56.

*In a letter to the author, Mr. Henry Baker Reiley, of Somerset, Pennsylvania, a descendant of Cornelius Reiley, states that his forebear took up a tract of land in Black Township in Somerset County in 1775, where the home was established in which James and Tobias Reiley were reared. Of that home the Rev. James Reiley, in his manuscript journal now in the possession of Mr. Reiley, of Somerset, says: "My father's house became a stopping place for the Heralds of the Cross; in addition, it being central between three places where they preached and had classes, and there being no other Methodist family near, it became a place of great resort for the members of the church."

James Wakefield, a local preacher on Black Lick Creek. They then turned westward to find an open door at the home of the father of James Wakefield on Chestnut Ridge. As they went they preached wherever an opportunity was offered along a course which took them down the westward slopes of Chestnut Ridge, along the Conemaugh, and across the Kiskiminitas in the vicinity of Saltsburg. Upon their arrival at Jacob's Creek, the Mason and the Ragan families opened their homes for services, and on a farm belonging to Zachariah Connell, grandfather of the preacher of that same name, divine worship was held on the present site of Connellsville.

Lurton and Matthews were venturesome men who felt at home on new trails, and were neither intimidated nor discouraged by the worst that the frontier could offer. In 1788 they drove the stakes of Zion along a greatly extended border, and in the spring of 1789, since no Conference was designated for Uniontown, they, with their co-workers in Western Pennsylvania, attended the Conference in Baltimore, which convened on May 4.

Since Charles Conaway reported no accessions for the Pittsburgh Circuit that year, it is apparent that progress was slow. His return to the circuit with a junior preacher in the person of Pemberton Smith, however, indicates that his work was satisfactory and that the field was promising. Richard Pearson and Thomas Carroll were his neighboring workers over on the Ohio Circuit, and to the Redstone Circuit came John Simmons and Nicholas Sebrell. The ablest leaders were Henry Willis and Lemuel Green, who served jointly as Presiding Elders. Willis was one of the gentlest and most highly cultured, yet aggressive and tireless itinerants of his day. Perhaps no other preacher held a place so secure in the affections and the confidence of Bishop Asbury as did he. He was the first preacher ordained by the Bishop after coming into his episcopal office, and it is doubtful if he ever placed his hands in consecration upon a worthier recipient. Henry Willis married Ann Hollingsworth, daughter of a leading Baltimore merchant, and when his health was broken by incessant labors, settled down on a six-hundred-acre farm near the site of the old Strawbridge meeting house in Maryland. It was her brother, F. Hollingsworth, who edited Asbury's Journals. When an epidemic made it impossible to hold the Conference of 1801 in Baltimore, Willis invited that body of forty men to his spacious home in the beautiful Wakefield Valley. After the death of Willis in 1808, Bishop Asbury passed that way a number of times, but never without visiting the grave of his very dear friend. About him he gathered the widow and her six children and gave thanks for all lovely memories. "Ah, when shall I look upon thy like again?" he was heard to say as he turned from the grave.

Such were the character and the ability of one of the Presiding Elders to whom was entrusted the oversight of Methodism in western Pennsylvania in 1789. And his co-laborer Lemuel Green, the Marylander, who found a resting place in the burying grounds of old Union Church, Philadelphia, brought to his work acceptable qualifications.

On July 3 of this year Bishop Asbury left Philadelphia in company with Richard Whatcoat, making the rather pessimistic entry in his Journal:

"Twenty years have we laboured in Pennsylvania, and there are not one thousand in society; how many of these are truly converted God knows." On the eighteenth day they passed through Greensburg, successor to Hannastown a few miles north, which had been sown to blood and ashes by Indians in 1782. In the new seat of justice they stopped "at Hanover Davis's, a man who had had trouble and conviction: his three sons were killed by the Indians, his wife and two children taken prisoners, and detained from him for eighteen months." [10] The next day they dined at Rowletts, rode twenty-five miles, where he was to get his first glimpse of Pittsburgh. "There," he continues, "I preached in the evening to a serious audience. This is a day of very small things: what can we hope? yet what can we fear? I felt love to the people; and hope God will arise to help and bless them." On Monday, the following day, he preached with "some zeal, and the people were attentive; but alas! they are far from God, and too near the savages in situation and manners." At the Tuesday evening service matters improved, for whereas "The night before the rude soldiers were talking and dancing about the floor; but now they were quiet and mute; this, I judged, might be owing to the interference of the officers, or magistracy." A larger audience and better order caused the Bishop to confess, "I felt more courage."

Pittsburgh had not been overly hospitable to Methodism's first episcopal visitor. He says, "We were not agreeably stationed at ————, who was continually drunk, and our only alternate was a

---

[10] For the record of this visit, see Asbury's Journal, Vol. II, pp. 56, 57.

ALL ROADS LEAD FROM UNIONTOWN 71

tavern." Yet the town of several hundred log dwellings and shops was making progress in morals, manners, and enlightenment. The Bishop could read the latest news in the Pittsburgh *Gazette*, the first newspaper west of the Allegheny Mountains, a sheet ten by sixteen inches, which had been founded three years before by John Scull and Joseph Hall. The previous September Allegheny County had been created out of Westmoreland County, which prior to that time had comprised all of southwestern Pennsylvania. The rather spirited dispute was dying down over the location of county buildings following the report of a committee that the Northside, or Allegheny, was unfavorable as a site since "it abounds in high hills and deep hollows, almost inaccessible to a surveyor." The townsmen were still wondering how the four hundred emigrants of General Putnam whose boat, the *Mayflower*, had pushed off at West Newton on the Youghiogheny the summer before and had touched at Pittsburgh, en route to Marietta, were faring on the Ohio frontier.

On Wednesday, after a three-day sojourn in Pittsburgh, Bishop Asbury, with Lemuel Green, Henry Willis, and Charles Conaway, directed their course eastward along the Allegheny River "to Wilson's, who was formerly an elder in the Presbyterian Church." On Thursday his Journal records: "We had a number of poor, attentive people at M'G―――'s; the weather was excessively warm, and we were in a log house, without so much as a window to give us air." They attended a Quarterly Conference, probably at the home of Thomas Moore, near Connellsville, where they "had a shout amongst the people," and entered Uniontown, "where there appeared to be some melting love among the people."

The good Bishop had apparently revived from the doldrums into which he had lapsed in Philadelphia, for he writes of Uniontown: "Now I believe God is about to work in this place; I expect our circuits are better supplied than formerly; many of the people are alive to God, and there are openings in many places." In this changed mood the good Bishop wrote a sympathetic letter to the Seneca chieftain, Cornplanter, mounted his horse and disappeared over Laurel Hill, leaving as a parting testimony: "I have constant consolation, and do not feel like my former self." Apparently western Pennsylvania had done him good.

CHAPTER VI

WHEN FAITH FLAMED IN THE DARKNESS

BEFORE entering upon a review of the decade beginning with 1790, let us glance at the achievements since 1784, when two circuit riders sought to find their way along strange trails, to collect congregations where there were no meeting houses, and to enroll members where a Methodist classbook had never been opened. It is relatively easy to trace Methodism by the General Minutes, and they are an indispensable help. In them one hears the hoofbeats of the itinerant's horse along new paths, and sees circuits and Conferences rising up in the western wilderness like storied islands emerging in a phantom sea. The membership returns of those ancient circuits, however, are discouragingly incomplete. They contain but a small fragment of the story. When, therefore, in 1790 the circuits in western Pennsylvania report memberships of 97 for Pittsburgh, 334 for Redstone, and 260 for Ohio, the sacrificial labors and, above all, the promise of coming years, have entirely evaded the printer's ink.

The second Conference to meet in Uniontown convened on July 29, 1790. Of that Conference Bishop Asbury says: "It was conducted in peace and love."[1]

---
[1] For an account of this Conference, see Asbury's Journal, Vol. II, p. 92.

On Saturday, August 1, the Bishop preached on education. The theme was in keeping with the action taken that year to provide ampler Christian education for the young. Methodism had taken an advanced position committing itself to this program: "Let us labor, as the heart and soul of one man, to establish Sunday schools, in or near the place of public worship," and a committee had been authorized to prepare a proper textbook. In the home of Thomas Crenshaw in Hanover County, Virginia, Bishop Asbury had organized a Sunday school as early as 1786, which has led to the belief that he was the American pioneer in this field of religious instruction.[2] In Uniontown he again dwelt upon a favorite subject. On Sunday he ordained Charles Conaway, Isaac Lunsford, and George Callahan elders, and four deacons. That faith was beginning to flame in the darkness is borne out from the Bishop's Journal of that date. He writes: "Here there is a revival among preachers and people: some of the societies are much engaged with God, and after we have had a few more Conferences in Uniontown, I hope we shall drive Satan out, and have a glorious work."

The optimism which possessed the Bishop at Uniontown seems to have been felt throughout the Church. Jesse Lee states: "We admitted on trial this year sixty-eight young preachers, and added to the society 14,365 members. There were more added to the society this year, than ever had been added before in the course of one year."[3] It was in such an atmosphere of encouragement that the

---

[2] See Finley, James B., Autobiography of, p. 389.

[3] Lee, Jesse, "A Short History of the Methodists in the United States of America," pp. 160, 161.

Conference held its sessions and the preachers turned to their appointments. Charles Conaway entered upon the presiding eldership with all of western Pennsylvania, Ohio, and the major part of the present state of West Virginia on his district. To the Randolph Circuit, included on his district, was appointed Anthony Banning, a Connellsville boy.

George Callahan, who was sent to the Pittsburgh Circuit that year, had been but three years in the itinerancy, but he had already demonstrated his nerve in frontier fields. In September, 1787, he had been sent to Ohio. An episode of his career there is thus described: "Rev. George Callahan, a Methodist preacher traveling the Ohio Circuit, lying in Virginia between Wheeling and Pittsburgh, was probably the first man to enter Ohio, and had the honor of preaching the first Methodist sermon. He was invited to preach at Carpenter's Station, where a blockhouse was erected to protect the frontier settlements. On reaching the place he found a congregation already assembled. 'Fifteen or twenty hardy backwoodsmen,' says Samuel W. Williams, 'armed with rifles, tomahawks, and scalping knives, stood on the outside of the assembly as protectors against an alarm. After the sermon was ended, a pressing invitation was given the preacher to visit Carpenter's Fort again, and he cheerfully acceded to the request.' "[4]

The junior preacher appointed to the Pittsburgh Circuit in 1790 was Joseph Doddridge. He was born in a community known as Friend's Cove, south of Bedford, Pennsylvania, in 1769. His father,

---

[4] Barker, John Marshall, "History of Ohio Methodism" (Cincinnati, New York, 1898), pp. 82, 83.

John Doddridge, there, as later in Washington County, was one of the most influential Methodist laymen of western Pennsylvania. A brother of John, Philip Doddridge, after three of his children had been carried into captivity with their grandmother and a cousin, and their grandfather scalped by Indians on Dunkard Creek in 1778, later with the mother and remaining child took up his residence near his kinsmen in Washington County. The fate of the grandmother is unknown, but the three daughters were carried to Detroit where one died, another was sold to a French officer and as his wife was taken to France, and the third married White Eyes, greatest chieftain of the Delaware nation, and declined all importunities to forsake her tawny captors. Philip Doddridge was a devoted helper of the infant society in Washington County, and after he moved to Indiana in 1818 with his wife and five children, his family became notable in Methodism. A son, John, became an exhorter, and for him Doddridge's Chapel, six miles south of Fort Wayne, was named.[5] Owing to the death of his father in 1791, Joseph Doddridge withdrew from the Methodist ministry, entered Jefferson Academy at Canonsburg, Pennsylvania, and subsequently devoted his life to the profession of medicine and the ministry of the Protestant Episcopal Church. Of his brother, the Honorable Philip Doddridge, who occupied a place of national prominence in politics, and was a leader in Methodism in Brooke County, West Virginia, a part of the Redstone Circuit, Jacob Young says, "He was, perhaps, the greatest man I ever knew."[6]

---

[5] See Doddridge, Joseph, "Notes on the Settlement and Indian Wars," pp. 278-281. Also Smith, William C., "Indiana Miscellany," pp. 102, 103.

[6] Young, Jacob, "Autobiography of a Pioneer" (Cincinnati, 1857), p. 277

During 1790 Daniel Fidler extended the work on the Ohio Circuit, and to the Redstone Circuit Amos G. Thompson and Thomas Haymond were appointed. The latter was a son of Caleb Haymond, a pioneer Methodist who lived south of Clarksburg, West Virginia. He has been described as "an amiable, sweet-spirited, holy man of God, and a powerful preacher; a man of great simplicity, and much beloved by the people."[7] James Quinn parted with Thomas Haymond after they had spent the night of June 1, 1799, in the home of Thomas Spahr. He writes: "We parted next morning to meet no more on earth; for on the 13th of that month, at the house of Caleb Pumphrey, his happy, blood-washed spirit took its flight to paradise, and his body was entombed in the Methodist burying-ground, at Cadesh Chapel, midway betwen Wellsburg and West Liberty, Brook County, Va., where not a stone tells where he lies. But I was told a few years ago, that a lovely elm had sprung up on or near his grave. Lovely man, I loved him much; and when I heard of his death, I tried to pray that the Lord would give me his mantle, if it had not fallen on some other."[8]

The schedule of Conferences for 1791 included one to be held at Uniontown, on July 28. That date, however, found Bishop Asbury nearing Albany, New York, after a swing through New England. At the Conference in New York the previous spring, after a private interview of three hours, Jesse Lee had induced Bishop Asbury to send preachers into New England.[9] Doubtless in 1791 Lee so presented the urgency of an episcopal visit to that new and

---
[7]Smith, Henry, "Recollections and Reflections of an Old Itinerant," p. 35.
[8]Wright, John F., "Sketches of the Life and Labors of James Quinn," p. 46.
[9]Thrift, Minton, "Memoir of the Rev. Jesse Lee," p. 161.

difficult field that the Bishop elected to spend the summer there rather than in the West.

That year the preachers in Western Pennsylvania were saddened with the news that John Wesley had died on March 2. Despite the reluctance of Mr. Wesley to surrender his personal supervision over them, and the fact that they had dropped his name from the Discipline, they had not dropped him from their hearts. Bishop Asbury wrote, "For myself, notwithstanding my long absence from Mr. Wesley, and a few unpleasant expressions in some of the letters the dear old man has written to me (occasioned by misrepresentation of others), I feel the stroke most sensibly." Turning to a consideration of Mr. Wesley's extraordinary abilities, he left this estimate of him: "So much of the spirit of government in him; his knowledge as an observer; his attainments as a scholar; his experience as a Christian; I conclude, his equal is not to be found among all the sons he hath brought up, nor his superior among all the sons of Adam he may have left behind."[10] And so wherever Methodists of the Redstone, Pittsburgh, and Ohio Circuits congregated that summer, their conversation was of Mr. Wesley. He had laid the foundations of their Church in the New World, sent missionaries to them, among whom was Bishop Asbury, and had devised a polity that had sent circuit-riders to the remotest cabins.

In 1791 Amos G. Thompson, who had served the Redstone Circuit the preceding year, was appointed Presiding Elder of the work in Western Pennsylvania, and Daniel Fidler and James Coleman were sent as his successors. Among the trophies won to the Church under their ministry the following spring

---

[10] Asbury's Journals, Vol. II, p. 115.

was a diffident Fayette County youth of seventeen who rode regularly from his home near Uniontown to services held in the spacious home of Colonel John Beck, three miles east of West Liberty on Long Run, Ohio County, West Virginia. One evening after James Coleman had preached, young Quinn arose from his accustomed seat on a chest behind the door, and approaching the preacher said, "I wish to join your church, if there are no objections."[11] Whatever other success may have come to Fidler and Coleman that year, the enlistment of James Quinn was an achievement of no inconsiderable worth to the cause of Western Methodism through half a century.

Charles Conaway, who had led the way into Pittsburgh in 1788, was returned to the Pittsburgh Circuit for the third time in 1791. The work on the Ohio Circuit was carried on by William McLenahan and Thomas Haymond. McLenahan arrived in America from Ireland at the age of nineteen, and by 1787 had entered upon the career of an itinerant in which he heroically passed through many deprivations. For forty-five years he shared in the extension of Methodism, although in his latter years in a supernumerary or retired relationship in the Philadelphia Conference. At his death, July 10, 1834, the following tribute was paid to him, "Retiring in his manners, humble in his disposition, deeply pious, and zealously devoted to his work, he acquired and maintained the confidence of his brethren, and commended himself to every man's conscience in the sight of God."[12]

---
[11] Wright, John F., "Sketches of the Life and Labors of James Quinn," pp. 23, 24.

[12] "Minutes of the Annual Conferences, 1773-1839," Vol. II, p. 348.

Chapter VII
"SO MIGHTILY GREW THE WORD OF GOD AND PROSPERED"

THE year 1792 proved to be one in which the hitherto feeble followers of John Wesley came into wider recognition in Western Pennsylvania, and began rearing the superstructure of a permanent institution upon the foundations which had been laid during a decade of patient and unheralded endeavor. That spring Bishop Asbury had followed the dim traces that threaded their way through the wilderness of Tennessee and Kentucky. In the Crab Orchard region it had been necessary, because of hostile Indians, to travel with convoys in one of which were as many as thirty-six armed frontiersmen. Riding with Bishop Asbury and sharing the dangers and hardships was the brave and consecrated Wilson Lee, to whom Methodism owes so much. "I walked the encampment, and watched the sentries the whole night," is the Bishop's description of how, in one place, he spent the time from dusk to dawn. As he rode northward through the present state of West Virginia he found the settlers so crowded in forts for defense against the savages that no comfortable sleeping places were available. His horse was jaded from travel, and weak from lack of feed and annoyance by flies. In lines that breathe both fatigue and gratitude, one reads in his Journal of Thursday, May 31, 1792: "Both men and horses traveled sore and wearily to Uniontown. O how good are clean houses, plentiful tables, and populous villages, when compared with the rough world we have come through! Here I turned out our poor horses to pasture and to rest, after riding them nearly three hundred miles in eight days."[1]

How the work had fared during his long absence we have scant knowledge. We do know how he felt about the matter, for a little more than two weeks before he arrived in Uniontown he wrote, "I am sensible the Western parts have suffered by my absence." The day following his arrival the Bishop "wrote letters to send over the mountains." Since the autumn of 1786, when John Scull became postmaster at Pittsburgh, a postal service had been operated between the forks of the Ohio and Philadelphia. Letters were not all that Bishop Asbury had concluded should be sent "over the mountains." "I found it necessary," he says in his Journal, "to remove, by exchange, six of the preachers from this to the Eastern district." This was not a sudden decision arising from an emergency. Weeks before while in the South he had expressed himself as being "more than ever convinced of the need and propriety of Annual Conferences, and of greater changes among the preachers."

There is a touch of sadness in the Bishop's description of his feelings at Uniontown. He was no longer young, and the exposures lately endured out on the rim of civilization had aggravated his rheumatic condition. "I have had some awful thoughts lest my

---

[1]For the account of Bishop Asbury's visit to western Pennsylvania in 1792, see his Journal, Vol. II, pp. 152, 153.

lameness should grow upon me, and render me useless," is a line written during the Conference session. Due to his illness he was obliged to absent himself from the preaching services, except on Sunday when he "ventured in public," and "a great crowd of people attended, and there was some melting and moving among them." His conscience, also, appeared to be giving him a little trouble as is indicated in this confession: "I sometimes have fears that I am too slack in speaking in public, at Conferences." Bishop Asbury was possessed of a hearty humor, enjoyed jovial companions, and seldom failed to contribute his full share to the sum of wholesome levity. Usually, however, such occasions were followed by periods of self-examination, which seemingly never failed to produce a like amount of remorse and self-reproach. Had his Journals been written at the table, about the fireside, or in the Conference session, rather than in periods of solitude and heart-searching, they might have escaped more of the shadows.

At Uniontown he also bemoaned the lack of opportunity, due to incessant travel, "to pursue," as he says, "my practice of solitary prayer." Freeborn Garrettson said of Bishop Asbury, "He prayed the best, and he prayed the most of any man I ever heard." One reads between the lines of the Bishop's account of the Conference that there were factors which troubled him other than the deprivation of opportunity for private devotions. "I feel the death of this district; I see what is wanting here—discipline," and he adds, "I have been variously tried, and was constrained to be cheerful." Bishop Asbury had a colossal capacity for work, handled details with dispatch and ease, but in presiding over a Conference he came, in his latter years, to rely more upon his position as a spiritual father over his children than upon the more rigid one of a disciplinarian. Not until the election of Bishop McKendree did the administration of an Annual Conference assume that orderliness of procedure by which deliverance from troubles present, and those to come, were appreciably minimized. Whether it was the difficulty encountered in working out an exchange between six men of the west with as many from the east, the records do not state, but the contrast between his account of the Conference this year and the previous one, indicates that Bishops even in that distant day experienced both shadow and sunshine.

There was inaugurated at this Conference in Uniontown in the summer of 1792 an enterprise which indicates that Bishop Asbury and his little company of circuit-riders were not solely pioneers in evangelism. An excerpt from the Bishop's Journal shows how, having sensed an urgent need, they ventured into the field of education. Of the beginning of this, the first institution of any sort to which Methodism directed its efforts in Western Pennsylvania, Bishop Asbury has written: "We have founded a seminary of learning called Union School. Brother C. Conway is manager, who also has charge of the district; this establishment is designed for instruction in grammar, languages, and the sciences."

James Hadden, the Uniontown historian, is of the opinion that the Baptists had founded an earlier academy on the site of the present village of Hopwood.* There are records to show that on July 31,

---

*For an account of the origin and development of the successive educational institutions that seemingly arose from the foundations laid by Charles Conaway, see Hadden, James, "A History of Uniontown" (Uniontown, 1913), pp. 483-518.

1794, Henry Beeson conveyed to Charles Conaway and other trustees a tract of land adjoining the old Methodist burying ground on West Peter Street, Uniontown. Although it was specified that this was to be the site of the Union District School, for some time the seminary was maintained in a room added to the original log Church. There the lamp of learning was lifted in the wilderness by Charles Conaway and his associates. Only the names of two or three of the school masters remain. Who the students were who stared curiously when funeral days came to the nearby burying ground, or followed with the longings of youth the cavalcades of traders and emigrants that moved along the Old Pike, or found recesses spent over at Beeson's Mill more to their liking than study periods in Charles Conaway's schoolroom—who these learners were, with the exception of a few to be noticed later, we shall never know.

We do know, however, that more than a century after Charles Conaway began meeting classes in his one-room "seminary," an institution still survived on the site of Madison College which was related, somewhat remotely it is true, to the humble pioneer institution mentioned by Bishop Asbury. Thirty-five years after the first venture of Methodism to found a seminary in Uniontown, the Pittsburgh Conference assumed control of Madison College. Six months passed in preparation, and on September 15, 1827, an impressive inaugural ceremony was held. An academic procession formed at the Methodist Episcopal Church, moved along the Old Pike across the bridge that spans Redstone Creek, and climbed the hill to the new college building which stood where the Church of St. John the Baptist now stands.

Although the history of Madison College belongs to a later period than that under review in this volume, there are certain facts regarding location, and continuity of interest, which link the later endeavor to that of the pioneers. The founders of that first school were men who had received but little formal education. They knew the value of learning not so much through possession as through deprivation. A contrast between the founders of 1792 and those of 1827 might be made with no reflection on the former. In passing, however, we shall take only a glance at two members of the faculty as, on an autumn day in 1827, they marched in procession through the streets of Uniontown to their waiting classrooms. Henry B. Bascom, the newly elected president, although but thirty-one years of age, had already served as Chaplain of the House of Representatives, and was nationally known as a pulpit orator. He was to become one of the most distinguished members of the College of Bishops of the Methodist Episcopal Church, South. Charles Elliott, professor of languages, was a young scholar from Ireland who had already impressed the Church with his erudition. His usefulness and ability were to find enlarged fields in the editorship of the *Pittsburgh Conference Journal*, the *Western*, and the *Central Christian Advocates*.

The next year an Ohio youth of seventeen walked over the hills of Western Pennsylvania with Madison College as his destination. His name was Matthew Simpson. Of this lad's childhood, Henry Boehm, traveling companion of Bishop Asbury, relates an interesting incident. Mr. Boehm writes, "In 1811, when traveling with him [the Bishop] near Xenia, Ohio, we were kindly entertained by a family named Simpson, and Bishop Asbury baptized a little infant and called him Matthew."[2] Although in after years Bishop Simpson was unable to confirm the claim of Mr. Boehm, there was one experience that stood out in his memory with the clarity of Laurel Hill as it rose before him in the clear air of 1827. Long afterward in reminiscent mood he wrote: "Uniontown was over ninety miles from Cadiz . . . my resources were narrow; I thought it best to make the journey on foot. So, tying my clothes and a few books in a little bundle which I carried, I set out for college with eleven dollars and twenty-five cents in my pocket." And a classmate of Bishop Simpson's was William Hunter, editor of the *Pittsburgh Christian Advocate*, and author of many hymns, among the best known of which to an earlier generation were "The Great Physician Now Is Here," and "My Heavenly Home Is Bright and Fair."

Strangest of all characters to enter Madison College was Henry Clay Dean, a foundling, who after being admitted to the Fayette County bar, abandoned it for the pulpit. He became one of Virginia's most eloquent Methodist preachers, but when the Church divided over the slavery issue, Dean, with his preaching ardor dampened, drifted into Iowa and settled on a one-thousand-acre farm. His vitriolic denunciation of Lincoln led to his being driven from Iowa to Missouri, where he named his large estate "Rebel's Cove," and became one of the most notable criminal lawyers of that state. In 1855 he served as Chaplain of the United States Senate. As far as is known, Mr. Dean never gave his reason for leaving Pennsylvania, but he did for leaving Iowa,

---

[2]Henry Boehm, "Reminiscences, Historical and Biographical" (New York, 1865), p. 446.

and so far as the Methodist Episcopal Church was concerned it would seem that he had also walked off the denominational reservation. He summed up the reasons that led to his leaving Iowa in these words: "The Black Republicans came into power in Iowa; they enacted the nefarious prohibition law, there was whisky gone; they abolished capital punishment, there was hanging gone; now they are drifting into Universalism, there is hell gone. I will not live in a state that does not believe in whisky, hanging, and hell."[3]

This excursion into the history of Madison College has led us into a field rather remote in time from 1792, and in kind, if we compare Bishop Asbury and Henry Clay Dean. Yet this flame of learning lighted in Uniontown so long ago cannot be ignored. As has been shown, it alternately flared with hope, and flickered with despair, but for over a century Cumberland Presbyterians, Methodist Protestants, and independent educators never quite allowed to be extinguished the flame which was kindled by Bishop Asbury, Charles Conaway, and their associates long, long ago.

We now return to the session of the Conference in Uniontown in 1792, that we may follow the preachers to their appointments. Amos G. Thompson was continued as Presiding Elder of the Redstone Circuit. William McLenahan, whom we met on the Ohio Circuit, was appointed to the Redstone Circuit, and with him went Jacob Peck as the junior preacher. Peck gave but two years to the ministry, and the glimpse given us of him by James Reiley at a camp meeting on the Greenbrier District in 1810 indicates that he had lapsed from his former useful

[3] Hadden, James, "History of Uniontown, Pennsylvania," p. 805.

state. Mr. James Reiley says: "At this meeting I saw Jacob Peck, a man who when young frequented my father's house as an itinerant, when I was quite a boy. But, O! he was deeply fallen. How did my poor heart yearn over him."[4]

No Methodist preacher had appeared in Western Pennsylvania who commanded so much attention as did Valentine Cook, who in 1792 was appointed to the Pittsburgh Circuit. Cook was born in the present Monroe County, West Virginia, in 1765, divided the spare time of his youth between his books and his rifles, and then set off for Cokesbury College from which he returned as perhaps the first native college-bred Methodist preacher to be heard in this region.

It seems that in making the rounds of his circuit Mr. Cook was charged not only with poaching unduly on the preserves of the Rev. Samuel Porter, who had been installed as the minister of the Congruity Presbyterian Church in 1790, but of disseminating doctrines which were subversive of the teachings of John Calvin. A word battle between Cook and Porter was carried on for some time in the press. A formal challenge to debate the main controversial differences between Calvinism and Arminianism was received from Samuel Porter by Valentine Cook. The exact time and place of the debate have been variously reported, but according to the records of the Trustees' Minute Book of the Congruity Congregation, the date was Wednesday, June 12, 1793, and the place "a few miles distant from Greensburg in some outdoor woodland where a great number of seats had been prepared, and a pulpit erected, and where, when the time arrived, 'a

---
[4]From the manuscript "Journal of James Reiley."

vast concourse of people were in attendance,' some of whom came over fifty miles."[5] For some reason the Rev. John Jamison was substituted for Samuel Porter. Jamison and Cook met for the first time on the grounds. Cook was rather tall, spare, stooped, with deep-set hazel eyes, and hair so black and straight that once when taken captive by Indians he was set at liberty, being mistaken by them for one of their own race. Nor did Cook's age, which then was twenty-seven, heighten Mr. Jamison's regard for his antagonist, which was already pretty low.

The controversy now belongs to a day that is dead. It is difficult from this remote date to conceive of so much enthusiasm, intolerance, and conviction enlivening the subject debated by Cook and Jamison. Anthony Banning rode over from Connellsville and sat beside Cook on a log while the settlers from far and near were assembling in the grove near the Congruity Church. Robert R. Roberts arrived from Ligonier, and judged from the talk about the grounds that the outlook for Cook was not very promising. The debate, however, made Cook a hero. For a generation that forest arena where Cook trounced Jamison became for Methodists what Braddock's Field was to the French and Indians. After a generous deduction is made for contemporary boasting, which is rather difficult to reconcile to the avowed humility of the founding fathers, it must be admitted that, although the debate settled no theological questions, it did have two rather wholesome effects on early Methodism. In the first place its doctrines had been

---
[5]"Trustees Minutes of Congruity Congregation" to September 25, 1893, pp. 1, 2. This information was furnished by Miss Mary Elizabeth Bierer, author of "Methodism in Greensburg," who has unearthed many interesting facts concerning this celebrated discussion.

placed before the people of Western Pennsylvania in such a masterly way that ever afterward they commanded more respect. In the second place, after Valentine Cook had finished off John Jamison in such an effective manner, and had sent Samuel Porter scurrying to his study to issue a printed polemic in an attempt to retrieve the day, the intellectual contempt in which the circuit-riders had been formerly held by a carefully trained ministry was noticeably changed.

The reputation established by Valentine Cook near Congruity was not so much that of a controversialist as that of an evangelist. James Quinn was of the opinion that it was Cook who first introduced the mourner's bench as an article of camp-meeting equipment. He says: "The first I ever heard of it was in 1795 or '96, at a watch-night held at the house of that mother of our Israel, the widow Mary Henthorn, near Uniontown, Penn. The person who conducted the meeting was that holy, heavenly minded man, the Rev. Valentine Cook — blessed man!" After describing Cook the writer proceeds: "He was not handsome; but when he conversed on the subject of religion—and it was almost his constant theme—and more especially when he preached, there was a sweet and almost heavenly benignity beaming in his countenance, presenting rather an unearthly attraction. It was next to impossible for the most heedless to remain uninterested under the sound of his voice."[6]

By 1800 Valentine Cook's health was in so precarious a state, due to hardships undergone in the itinerancy, that he was obliged to locate. In Ken-

---

[6] Wright, John F., "Sketches of the Life and Labors of James Quinn," pp. 205, 206.

tucky he served for a time as principal of Bethel Academy, second educational institution established by Methodists in America. As he advanced in years his reputation, earned in the more dramatic days of his ministry, suffered no diminution. In 1819 he visited the scenes of his Pennsylvania ministry. Twenty-five years had witnessed the widening into roads of the dim traces he had once followed to the frontier settlements, the erection of houses of worship where in his day none stood, and the replacement of those primitive log meeting-houses with substantial and commodious churches. It had been three years since Bishop Asbury rode for the last time down the eastern slopes of the Allegheny Mountains and found, on March 31, 1816, in the home of George Arnold near Spottsylvania, Virginia, the final rest he so often anticipated. Over at Congruity, the Rev. Samuel Porter, grown too feeble to stand, preached from a chair to the congregation, in whose esteem he gradually rose across thirty-five years. Through scenes that awakened old memories, into homes that had once extended their hospitality, and to the old preaching places that had once felt his power, Valentine Cook passed during his farewell tour in 1819. Thus on the way to his grave, which was but a few months distant, Valentine Cook returned to Kentucky from Pennsylvania laden with assurances of the confidence and the love of his parishioners of other years.

It is worthy of mention that the junior preacher appointed with Valentine Cook to the Pittsburgh Circuit in 1792 was Seely Bunn. He was born in Poughkeepsie, New York, in 1765, but spent his young manhood in Berkley County, Virginia, where, under the preaching of the itinerants, he was converted, and in 1792 was received into the traveling connection. Jesse Lee has thrown some light upon the physical dimensions of Seely Bunn. Upon the adjournment of the Conference in Baltimore on May 4, 1799, Mr. Lee wrote in his Journal: "After we had finished our business in Conference, four of the largest preachers amongst us went to a friend's store, and were weighed. My weight was 259 lbs. Seely Bunn's 252, Thomas Lucas' 245, and Thomas F. Sergent weighed 220; in all 976 lbs. A *wonderful* weight for four Methodist preachers, and all of us travel on horseback." [7] Seely Bunn was to remain in the saddle until 1814, and despite his heavy strain on horseflesh, was to ride circuits that seemed to specialize in rough roads and inhospitable savages. There is no record of the number of horses that succumbed under the weight of this circuit-rider, but strangely enough, as if to be spared any semblance of revenge, death came to Mr. Bunn, in 1834, when he fell from a gig. [8]

When Bishop Asbury read the appointments at Uniontown in 1792, Isaac Lunsford, Lasley Matthews, and Daniel Hitt constituted the triumvirate to carry the standards of Methodism over the Ohio Circuit. We met Lunsford on the occasion of his ordination to elder's orders by Bishop Asbury at Uniontown on August 2, 1790, and Matthews during his association with Jacob Lurton in extending the borders of the Redstone Circuit in 1788. Although Daniel Hitt arrived a stranger to this region in 1792, he was destined to become more familiar with it through a quarter of a century of association in

---

[7] Thrift, Minton, "Memoir of the Rev. Jesse Lee," p. 249.

[8] For obituary, see "Minutes of the Annual Conferences, 1773-1839," Volume II, p. 279.

some capacity than did almost any other preacher. The Hitt family of Fauquier County, Virginia, was among the first and most devoted in Methodism during the years of opposition and struggle. When on February 23, 1808, Bishop Asbury was a guest in this home, long one of his favorite stopping-places, he made this entry in his Journal: "For some days we have rested under the roof of Herman Hitt: he is now eighty-six. He has lived to see four generations. He is the head of eighteen families. Three of his sons are preachers, Martin, Daniel, and Samuel, and his grandson William also."[8]*

Daniel Hitt remained in Western Pennsylvania until the year 1801. During that period he spent a year on the Pittsburgh and two years on the Redstone Circuits, and received three appointments as Presiding Elder over a region that embraced parts of Ohio, Pennsylvania, and Virginia. During 1807 he acted as the traveling companion of Bishop Asbury. How firmly he established himself in the confidence of the Bishop is shown in this entry in the Journal at Winchester, New Hampshire, June 6, 1813: "Knowing the uncertainty of the tenure of life, I have made my will, appointing Bishop McKendree, Daniel Hitt, and Henry Boehm, my executors. If I do not in the meantime spend it, I shall leave, when I die, an estate of two thousand dollars, I believe: I give it all to the Book Concern."[9] The fact that from 1808 to 1816 Daniel Hitt was a Publishing Agent of the Book Concern, during whose administration Asbury

---

[8]"Asbury's Journals," Volume III, p. 276.

*A grandson of Martin Hitt, Robert Roberts Hitt, born at Urbana, Ohio, in 1834, emigrated to Illinois, where at the invitation of Abraham Lincoln he became the official reporter of the Lincoln-Douglas debates. Robert Roberts Hitt spent seven years as secretary of the legation in Paris, was Assistant Secretary of State with Blaine, and during the twenty years prior to his death, in 1906, was a member of Congress from Illinois.

[9]"Asbury's Journals," Volume III, p. 413.

made the institution his beneficiary, indicates a sustained confidence in Daniel Hitt's business ability. In 1820 Mr. Hitt was again laboring among the scenes of his early ministry west of the Allegheny Mountains as Presiding Elder of the Monongahela District. In 1825 this servant of the Church, to whom Methodism is so deeply indebted, died of typhoid fever, was buried in Washington County, Pennsylvania, but due to faulty reporting, his memoir contains no mention of either the exact place or date of his death or interment.[10]

On June 13, 1792, Bishop Asbury disappeared beyond the rim of Laurel Hill in none too happy a frame of mind, as we have seen. Out of the vexations of the Conference, however, two benefits had risen. A school had been established at Uniontown, and such able recruits as Valentine Cook and Daniel Hitt had been dispatched to man the local circuits. Not until 1796 did Bishop Asbury return to Western Pennsylvania, but it is likely that some of the preachers who were at Uniontown in June saw him at the General Conference which met in Baltimore on the first of the following November.

---

[10] See "Minutes of the Annual Conferences, 1773-1839," Volume I, p. 507.

CHAPTER VIII
LENGTHENING TRAILS AND RECEDING HORIZONS

BY THE summer of 1793 there were unmistakable signs that the settlers of the Redstone Country had gained mastery not only over the savages, but over those obstacles of a frontier noted for its challenging mountains and rivers. Since 1790, when only six freight-laden Conestoga wagons could be seen creeping precariously between Pittsburgh and Philadelphia, the number had so increased as to crowd from the road almost entirely those long trains of pack-horses which, since 1760, had gone single file over the narrow paths. Four years had passed since James Hayden of Fayette County had conveyed by wagon over the Braddock Road from Hagerstown the first consignment of freight to Jacob Bowman of Brownsville. Roads, those sure harbingers of civilization, were opening, and the sound of the wagoner's whip and voice was evidence of an expanding commercial and social life.

Over at Brownsville during the summer of 1793, much talk centered about the fate of their erstwhile citizen, Colonel John Hardin, who had set off on a peace mission to the Miami Indian villages the previous December. Her neighbors remembered Jane Davies, Monongahela Valley girl, who had married

Colonel Hardin, and migrated with him to Kentucky in 1786. They had become the pioneers of Methodism in Washington County, Kentucky. The Hardin home was one of Bishop Asbury's favorite stopping places. He told the family of his visits to Western Pennsylvania and gave them what news he could of their former Fayette County friends. In his Journal for April 13, 1793, is this doleful entry: "From the quarterly meeting we came to Col. Hardin's. He has been gone some time, as a commissioner, to treat with the Indians; if he is dead, here is a widow and six children left. I cannot yet give him up for lost." [1]

Since no Conference was held in Uniontown in 1793, the preachers were obliged to attend either the Conference that convened in Oldtown, Maryland, on June 16, or in Baltimore on November 21. Inasmuch as Oldtown, near Cumberland, was much nearer and met earlier, it seems probable that the preachers from Western Pennsylvania assembled at that session. The Journal of Bishop Asbury reveals nothing other than this observation made at Oldtown: "We had no small consolation in uniting the brethren from three districts in Conference; whose names only were before known to each other." [2]

Charles Conaway was appointed Presiding Elder over a district that contained fourteen circuits. Many of them exceeded in size some Conferences of today. Seely Bunn and Thomas Bell were appointed to the Redstone Circuit. Bell, who had joined the itinerant ranks in 1790, came to the Redstone Circuit from the Frederick Circuit in Maryland. Dan-

---
[1] "Asbury's Journals," Volume II, pp. 192, 193.
[2] "Asbury's Journals," Volume II, p. 198.

iel Hitt was shifted from the Ohio to the Pittsburgh Circuit. Alward White was to receive his initiation into the itinerancy in riding over the hills near Pittsburgh with Daniel Hitt. After four years White located, to resume the work in 1819, and to continue as a member of the Philadelphia Conference until his death in Greensborough, Maryland, November 23, 1832.[3]

Thomas Scott, destined to a distinguished legal career, was appointed to the Ohio Circuit in 1793. Although but twenty-one years of age, he had already spent four years on Southern circuits. In June before he came North to the Ohio Circuit, he had been ordained elder by Bishop Asbury at the place of his birth in Allegany County, Maryland. The Ohio Circuit included the eastern part of the State of Ohio, a section which was infested by Indians. Included in the circuit was a strip of Western Pennsylvania. Here the Calvinists were considered rather troublesome. In that day the life of a Methodist circuit-rider was not just one sustained spiritual glow. There were adversaries.

James Quinn, whose reminiscences indicate that he gloried in a doctrinal battle quite as much as in a camp-meeting, has given the following account of a public debate that "took place in the town of Washington, Washington County, Penn., some time in 1793, when Rev. T. Scott—now of Chilicothe—was traveling Ohio Circuit, Va., which at that time included the town of Washington. It seems that Mr. S. had obtained leave, and had preached a few times in the court-house. He was then young, and of very youthful appearance; yet, young as he was, his youth was not to be despised;

[3]"Minutes of the Annual Conferences, 1778-1839," Volume II, p. 216.

for many attended, and became much interested in the young Methodist minister." After presenting the reasons that led the Rev. Mr. Welsh to publish "that on a set day he would publicly expose and refute the errors of Methodism," Mr. Quinn returns to his hero thus: "The youthful Scott, in nothing afraid of his adversaries, published that he would be there to defend Methodism as Scriptural truth. The day came; and not the court-house, but the court-yard, was filled with people, many of whom had come from afar." After a none-too-flattering account of Mr. Welsh's first onslaught, Mr. Quinn again beats the drum for his conquering hero thus: "Then came on the youthful Scott, with his Gospel sling and smooth stones. He used soft words, but there were hard arguments in the logical arrangement, and they sunk deeply lodged in the understanding and the heart. Time has told well of that day's work, and no doubt eternity will tell more."[4]

When Thomas Scott had finished his year on the Ohio Circuit, he responded to the request of Bishop Asbury to cast his lot in the wilds of Kentucky where William Burke, Francis Poythress, and Wilson Lee were doing such valiant work. It was while there he was married, and with great reluctance, because of the inadequacy of the ministerial stipend, followed the course of many other gifted men of that day in retiring from the traveling ministry. The General Conference of 1792 had set the annual salary of all Methodist preachers at sixty-four dollars, and traveling expenses, and a similar amount for their wives, "if they be in want of it." Thomas Scott studied law and in 1800 entered upon that pro-

---

[4]Wright, John F., "Sketches of the Life and Labors of James Quinn," p. 216.

fession in Chillicothe, Ohio. There he renewed his friendship with Edward Tiffin who, when a young physician, had been so impressed with a sermon preached by Scott in a grove near Charlestown, West Virginia, that he went to the preacher's lodgings and united with the Church, became a local preacher, and was ordained by Bishop Asbury. In 1803 Edward Tiffin was elected the first Governor of Ohio, and in 1810 Thomas Scott became Chief Justice of the Supreme Court of that State. Thomas Scott resided in Chillicothe for over half a century, devoting his later years to the compilation of memories of his life as an itinerant. Like that of Governor Tiffin, the Christian reputation of Judge Scott, though long exposed to politics, remained unsullied.

Robert Bonham, who traveled the Ohio Circuit with Thomas Scott in 1793, was a son of Hezekiah Bonham, the escort of Bishop Asbury on his first journey to the Redstone Country. As we have already seen, his escape from a falling sycamore limb during a service in a grove, caused him to bring charges of sinister intent against the devil. The faith of Robert Bonham had been kindled at those early altar fires lighted by Robert Strawbridge in Carroll County, Maryland. His ministerial career was cut short by a lingering illness to which he succumbed at Baltimore in June, 1800.[5]

The plan of episcopal visitation for 1794 included a Conference at Uniontown on June 12. The printed Journals of Bishop Asbury contain no entries between June 9, when he was a guest in the home of Elisha Phelps near Shepherdstown, Virginia, and June 17, when he was within a day's ride of Balti-

---

[5] For memoir, see Minutes of the Annual Conferences, 1773-1839, Volume I, pp. 91, 92.

more. Were those unprinted sections of the Journals, which fell prey to flames, available more light might be thrown on the progress of Methodism in Western Pennsylvania during the year 1794. We do know that the preachers were obliged to do their work in the midst of lawlessness and political excitement such as has never been seen since in this locality. In 1790, at the suggestion of Alexander Hamilton, a duty had been levied on domestic and imported liquors. Several Federal collectors, as well as distillers who ventured to pay the tax, had been tarred and feathered, or branded with hot irons; and persons who rented their property for the collectors' offices were not only boycotted socially, but did so at the risk of having their buildings destroyed. This reign of lawlessness, known as the Whisky Insurrection, reached its most alarming stage in the summer of 1794 when, led by Daniel Bradford and incited by the teachings of Citizen Genet, mobs attempted the life of General John Neville, burned his home, and assembled in vast numbers on Braddock's Field on August 1, 1794, for the purpose of making a destructive march on Pittsburgh. Not until President Washington sent Governor Henry Lee, of Virginia, up the Braddock Road at the head of 14,000 militiamen, were law and order restored.

It would be interesting to know just how the Methodist intinerants fared in the towns along the Monongahela and Youghiogheny Rivers where indignation reached white heat, and over in Washington County where night-riders were afield at every indication of a collector's arrival. This year Charles Conaway was appointed Presiding Elder of the Clarksburg, Ohio, Washington, Redstone, and Pittsburgh Circuits. Jesse Lee locates the Washington

Circuit "to the west of Baltimore," which saves one from the confusion of associating it with the county and town of that name in Western Pennsylvania. Charles Conaway's district was still large, although it had been greatly reduced from its former dimensions of empire.

In 1794 Daniel Hitt was placed in charge of the Redstone Circuit and John Phillips, an apprentice, was assigned to assist him. John Watson, who was appointed to the Pittsburgh Circuit this year, was not a man to court danger, but it is certain that he moved unafraid through the alarms of the Whisky Insurrection. Henry Smith has left an indication of the utter abandon with which Watson carried forward the Lord's cause. At the Conference held in Baltimore in October, 1795, the year John Watson closed his work on the Pittsburgh Circuit, Bishop Asbury asked for volunteers for Kentucky. Half a century later Smith recounted the circumstances in these words: "On the twenty-fifth I was ordained in a private home, before Conference opened; and in a few hours after my ordination John Watson and myself were on horseback, on our way to Kentucky, almost before anyone knew we were going."[6] There is a sentence so free from any consciousness of the dramatic or the heroic on the part of the writer, that it discloses how in that day men like Watson and Smith acted under the divine compulsion. "John Watson and myself were on horseback, on our way to Kentucky, almost before anyone knew we were going," is one of those occasional sentences upon which one comes in the chronicles of the old circuit-riders, which mirror their renunciation

---

[6]Smith, Henry, "Recollections and Reflections of An Old Itinerant," p. 87.

and daring. Over the Allegheny Mountains to the Youghiogheny River proceeded Watson and Smith. After weeks of waiting they embarked, with two families and thirteen horses, in a badly overcrowded boat. After nine days and nights of constant rowing through stormy winter weather, the boat docked and the two spiritual adventurers led their horses ashore, mounted them, and rode off to their circuits in the wilds of Kentucky. It was a man of that stamp that the Pittsburgh Circuit was fortunate enough to have minister to it during the years of 1794 and 1795. John Watson, a native of Maryland, but for thirty-three years at home in the itinerant's saddle, died near Martinsburg, West Virginia, in the summer of 1838.

Little is known of Richard Ferguson, the junior preacher on the Pittsburgh Circuit during the pastorate of Mr. Watson. The Minutes of 1796, however, indicate that his brethren felt that he had forfeited the privilege of continuing in the ministry. That he was restored to the favor of his friends and to a place of prolonged service in the Church is indicated from the following reference to his connection with Fell's Church: "The first local preacher, in the order of service, was Richard Ferguson, who was a local preacher for thirty-five years, and died in 1828 at the age of sixty. He seems to have been the junior preacher on the Pittsburgh Circuit in 1794-95. At the time of his death he was residing in another community, but was so warmly attached to Fell's Church and his friends in it, that he requested his body be buried at Fell's."[7]

To the Ohio Circuit in 1794 was appointed Samuel Hitt, son of the patriarchal Herman Hitt, of

---

[7]Craig, Blanche, "The First Fifty Years of Fell's Church," p. 8.

Fauquier, Virginia, and brother of Daniel, who at this same Conference was sent to the neighboring Redstone Circuit. We shall have occasion later to refer to John H. Reynolds, who shared with Samuel Hitt the work of the Ohio Circuit this year.

A study of the Minutes of the Annual Conferences of 1795 reveals certain omissions in appointments and statistics that were perhaps the result of an attempt to eliminate duplications in tabulating the returns of the Annual Conferences. We know that Henry Smith, who had spent an adventurous time down on the Clarksburg Circuit in 1794, served at least a part of 1795 on the Pittsburgh and the Redstone Circuits, although his name does not appear opposite these appointments. In fact the appointments of the five circuits that comprise this region west of the Allegheny Mountains are identical for 1794 and 1795, save that in the later year John H. Reynolds is down for the Union School at Uniontown, and Thomas Haymond appears as his successor on the Ohio Circuit.

It will be remembered that Bishop Asbury arrived at the Conference in Uniontown in 1792 "more than ever convinced of the need . . . of greater changes among the preachers," and true to his conviction he "found it necessary to remove, by exchange, six of the preachers from this to the eastern district." The Bishop's plan to make of Methodism a vast animated checkerboard is confirmed by the final paragraph of the printed Minutes for 1794. It reads: "N. B. The Bishop and Conference desire that the preachers would generally change every six months, by the order of the Presiding Elder, whenever it can be made convenient." [8]

---
[8]Minutes of the Annual Conferences 1773-1839, Volume I, p. 58.

Perhaps that explains the account of his experiences on the Pittsburgh and the Redstone Circuits during the year 1795 as given by Henry Smith, although his name, as has been stated, does not officially appear. On the first Sunday in May, 1795, Smith preached a farewell sermon as pastor of the Clarksburg Circuit in the courthouse in Morgantown. He says, "The time had now arrived when I must leave this circuit and go to Redstone." That this was in compliance with the six-month-shift order quoted above seems apparent from the following account: "I set out for my circuit; but, being requested by the Presiding Elder, I took one round on Pittsburgh Circuit, where I had some meetings, attended with great power. Good was done, and I was much encouraged to go forward. On the 28th I got orders to return to Redstone. But shortly after I got on the circuit my horse died. This was a cross to me, indeed, for I had no means of buying another. The means were, however, soon furnished by my kind friends on the circuit." Wherever he went in Western Pennsylvania, Henry Smith heard accounts "of the famous controversy between Mr. Cook and Messrs. Porter and Jameson," although three years had passed since the debate. At the time Mr. Smith was setting down his reminiscences of events that had transpired more than fifty years before, he turned aside to observe, "A copy of the first letter from Mr. Porter to Mr. Cook is in my possession."

Mr. Smith next pays a tribute to Thomas Haymond, preacher in charge of the Redstone Circuit, who, because of illness, had been obliged to relinquish his work. He says: "To lose such a colleague was no ordinary loss to me, for I was left alone, and in charge of a large circuit. I was young and inexperienced, and had disagreeable business to settle in some of the societies. . . . Our first quarterly meeting was held at Brother Roberts' in Leganeer (Ligonier) Valley, some time in July, and we had a glorious time. . . . Brother Hitt preached us one of his best sermons, and good was done. This Brother Roberts was the father of our worthy Bishop Roberts. In this pious family I had a pleasant time. Robert R. Roberts was then but a boy. . . . Little did I then think that he ever would be my bishop, and such a bishop as he has proved himself to be." [9]

Henry Smith was one of the most useful and respected ministers of his day. He was a lad in the home of his German father in Frederick County, Virginia, when Methodist preachers first appeared in the community. By a strange providence persons either then, or later, connected with the Redstone country began to direct the course of his life towards its great usefulness. For instance, of one of his helpers he writes: "Toward the fall of 1789, Sister Connell, grandmother of Zachariah Connell, of the Ohio Conference, came from beyond the Allegheny Mountains, on a visit to her friends in our neighborhood. She felt seriously concerned for her friends, and the neighborhood in which she had been brought up, and applied to my father to let the Methodist preachers preach in his house. Although I was a wild and thoughtless youth, I had no objection to have preaching there." [10] This is that same Mrs. Connell whom we have seen with her husband welcoming the weary itinerants, Jacob Lurton and

---

[9]Smith, Henry, "Recollections and Reflections of An Old Itinerant," pp. 33-36.

[10]Smith, Henry, "Recollections and Reflections of An Old Itinerant," p. 236.

Lasley Matthews to her cabin home to make of it a Bethel in the woods where Connellsville now stands. And when the next year, during a visit to her former home in Virginia, the father of Henry Smith yielded to Mrs. Connell's importunities to permit preaching in his house, among the first preachers invited was Thomas Scott, the seventeen-year-old circuit-rider who shortly would himself be heard in the preaching places of the Redstone country. Of that service Mr. Smith long afterward wrote, "Under the preaching of Thomas Scott (now Judge Scott of Ohio), I surrendered my heart to God, and in the name of Jesus resolved to be religious." Henry Smith died in 1863 at the age of almost ninety-four. He was a lovable character, long held in veneration by his brethren of the Baltimore Conference. In his later years he added a touch of other days by appearing in his circuit-rider's clericals at the Conference sessions, where he was always honored with a seat on the platform. He spent the evening of his life at "Pilgrim's Rest," near Baltimore, where, as he worked in his garden, he summoned out of the past the events of his long and dramatic life. Then he would put aside his spade and retire to his study to jot down the trooping memories. They first appeared as letters in *The Christian Advocate and Journal*, and were subsequently published in the volume, "Recollections and Reflections of an Old Itinerant."

In 1795 John H. Reynolds was appointed to Union School. The year previous he had been the junior preacher on the Ohio Circuit with Samuel Hitt. That Reynolds did not continue in the ministry is evident from the disappearance of his name from the Minutes after two years on the probationary list. James Quinn gives this account of the association of Reynolds with Union School and its early history: "The Uniontown school enterprise was gotten up in 1793 or 1794; but at whose instance I am not fully prepared to say. I think, most probably, that it originated with Mr. Asbury. However, most certain it is, that the good man took a lively interest in the project. A Mr. Sheppee, an Englishman, of considerable learning, was the first principal here. He, however, continued but a short time, and was succeeded by the Rev. John Hooker Reynolds, a Welshman, a traveling preacher on trial. He was appointed to Union School in 1795, and remained, say two years, as teacher of languages, while the English department was conducted by Rev. William Wilson, of Eastern Shore, Maryland. These were said to be competent men. But as this was a small concern, without charter or endowment, having to depend wholly on tuition fees for its support, it soon went down, and was abandoned, involving a few in pecuniary liability to some small amount. Short lived, however, as was this institution, it produced some literary fruit: two M.D.'s, Stevens and Boyd; one lawyer, T. Mason;[*] and two

---

[*]This reference is probably to Thomas Meason, son of Colonel Isaac Meason, a pioneer ironmaker of Western Pennsylvania. His mansion at Mount Braddock, built in 1802, still stands as one of the most impressive landmarks of Fayette County. There Bishop Asbury was a frequent guest of Colonel Meason whom he described as "one of the great men of the West." A daughter of Isaac Meason married Jacob Murphy, son of Mrs. Ann Murphy, and resided on lands adjoining Mount Braddock, originally a part of the Gist plantation. Mrs. Ann Murphy, a widow who came from Maryland, was perhaps the most influential among the founders of Methodism in Uniontown and vicinity. The devotion of this noble woman was continued in her son, Jacob Murphy. One finds his name among the trustees of two of the earliest Methodist churches in Fayette County. In his home in 1804 Bishop Asbury ordained William Page, elder, and Andrew Hemphill, deacon. Of the lawyer cited by Quinn as a product of Union School, we have this account: "General Thomas Meason, son of Isaac Meason, of the Mount Braddock farm, was admitted September 25, 1798, and left Uniontown in the winter of 1812-13 on horseback to enlist at Washington City in the service of his country, and caught cold on his journey which caused his death at the age of forty years. He was buried in the Congressional burying grounds. He read law with James Ross, of Pittsburgh." From "A History of Uniontown, Pennsylvania," by James Hadden, p. 408.

ministers of eminence, Rev. Thomas Lyel (Lyell)†
of the Protestant Episcopal Church, of New York,
and our dear S. Parker, of the West, received the
rudiments of a classical education at Union
School." [11]

The academy at Uniontown was not the only educational institution that gave Bishop Asbury anxiety in 1795. On December 7 of that year Cokesbury College, at Abingdon, Maryland, a school for which Methodist preachers in this section had been soliciting financial aid since the days of Cooper and Breeze, burned to the ground. Valentine Cook, of whom we have taken notice, was the most distinguished alumnus of Cokesbury College known to Methodists of Western Pennsylvania. It had been the dream of its founders that at Cokesbury College "learning and religion might go hand in hand." But from the beginning debt had been an intrusive third party. Rule eighteen of the college expressly forbade indulgence in play. "Let this rule be observed with the strictest nicety, for those who play when they are young will play when they are old," was the admonition of the grave trustees. There was recreation for the students, to be sure, but it was provided in the carpenter shop or the garden. It would be interesting to know whether there were fewer fires suspected of incendiary origin after

---

†Thomas Lyell was a Virginian who was received on trial in the itinerant ministry in 1791. He became the first chaplain of the House of Representatives after the establishment of the Federal Government in Washington in 1800. In 1804 Mr. Lyell entered the ministry of the Protestant Episcopal Church, and had a distinguished and useful career as rector of one of the prominent churches of New York City. An interesting sketch of Lyell when junior preacher on the Frederic Circuit, Virginia, with Thomas Scott in 1792, is given in "Sketches of Western Methodism," by James B. Finley, pp. 155, 156.

[11] Wright, John F., "Sketches of the Life and Labors of James Quinn," pp. 218, 219.

Methodist educators began modifying the rules on college recreation. One year to a day following the burning of Cokesbury College, several circuit-riders from west of the Allegheny Mountains were in Baltimore attending the General Conference in the Light Street Church. They heard the alarm of fire given, and saw not only the Church consumed in flames, but also the school next door which had been opened that autumn as the successor to Cokesbury College.

The year 1795 brought dismay not only to men like Bishops Asbury and Coke and John Dickins, who had dreamed their dreams of establishing a college almost before the soldiers of the Revolution had recovered from their wounds, but a thing the like of which Methodists had never before known, made its appearance. The year showed a decrease in membership. "We found our number of members," wrote Jesse Lee, "was less this year than it was last year. Such a loss of members we had never known since we were a people. There was a restless spirit in most parts of our connection and many were scattered by the division in the south of Virginia." [12]

Never, however, in more than a decade of missionary effort west of the Allegheny Mountains had men of higher ability and deeper consecration appeared than were found among those who went the rounds of their circuits in 1795. There was Charles Conaway, of tireless energy and abundant resourcefulness, supervising the district. Daniel Hitt had brought to the Redstone Circuit a rare blend of common sense and zeal. John Watson, who never took counsel of his fears, seemed a selection suitable

---
[12] Lee, Jesse, "A Short History of the Methodists," p. 26.

not only to the God-fearing, but to the rougher elements in the Pittsburgh Circuit, while over on the Ohio Circuit the Christian witness of Thomas Haymond, fast moving toward his grave, was that of a powerful light in a frail setting.

Chapter IX

A STRONG MAN COMES OVER THE MOUNTAINS

By 1796, a dozen years had passed since Francis Asbury, accompanied by Hezekiah Bonham, followed the Braddock Road northward to see how the wilderness preachers, John Cooper and Samuel Breeze, prospered in preparing the way of the Lord. The monuments to the labors of themselves and their successors were certainly not in the form of houses of worship, but rather in individuals who had been led to walk in newness of life, and in communities that had evidenced a heightened moral tone under the transforming power of the spoken word. Members of the societies in Western Pennsylvania doubtless accepted the recommendation made the previous year, "that the first Friday in March, 1796, should be held as a most solemn day of fasting, humiliation, prayer, and supplication," for individual and national sins. It was doubtless the decrease in membership that induced the leaders to catalogue the sins inimical to the progress of the Church, and to call for their renunciation on a day of general fasting.

The latter part of May, Bishop Asbury again directed his course northward to visit Methodism's outposts in the Upper Valley of the Ohio. In all his years of travel his animosity toward bad roads had never softened. Rocks, roots, and ruts were the old adversaries that waylaid him along all his Western journeys. "Ah! if I were young again!" he sighed as he contemplated the fatigue of crossing the Allegheny Mountains in 1796. A new trail where, he says, "We were in danger of being plucked off our horses by the boughs of the trees under which we had to ride," caused him to dub Tygart's Valley "The Valley of Distress." Daniel Hitt had ridden down to the Greenbriar country to accompany the Bishop into his district, a duty then incumbent upon Presiding Elders. The Bishop, however, voiced the state of his conscience thus, "I doubt whether I shall ever request any person to come and meet me at the levels of Greenbriar, or to accompany me across these mountains again, as Brother D. Hitt has now done."[1] No doubt when Daniel Hitt became his traveling companion in 1807, he often wished the Bishop's conscience would revert to its 1796 state of sensitiveness.

Bishop Asbury spent from the second to the thirteenth of June, 1796, in Western Pennsylvania. At one unnamed preaching place he "had half a dozen preachers and a congregation of serious hearers, and some wept." His Journal reads, "Thursday, 9. We crossed Great Yohogany, and came to Connel's Town where we had a good time." Of Mrs. Connell, whom he found ill, he says, "I gave her counsel and medicine, and trust I left her better in soul and body." Two days later he rode to Uniontown where he declares, "after a solemn meeting, I sat in Conference with the preachers." Two days later he rode through the narrow street of the village of Uniontown and was soon lost from view in the mountain forests.

---

[1] For the account of this visit, see Asbury's Journal, Volume II, p. 304.

Due to the appearance of a double list of appointments for Western Pennsylvania Circuits in the Minutes of the Annual Conference of 1796, it is difficult to determine whether the preachers were given their appointments at Uniontown or at Philadelphia, where all who regularly reported to the Baltimore Conference were instructed to be present on October 10, to be stationed. This was necessitated by the convening of the General Conference in Baltimore ten days later. At any rate we find Daniel Hitt appointed to the Presiding Eldership, and to the Redstone Circuit, Charles Conaway, Thomas Haymond, J. Fell, and James L. Higgins. Since John Fell's name appears for the first time in the appointments of this year, we present the following account of his conversion and call to the ministry as given by Miss Blanche Craig: "The year 1786 saw the Fell family comfortably settled in their new home at Fellsburg, as Benjamin's grant was called. On a certain Sunday of that year a congregation gathered at the home of Mrs. Casner, where the town of Donora now stands, to hear David Combs, a local preacher from Bucks County, who was on his way to Kentucky. . . . In the congregation were Benjamin Fell and his son John. The latter was amazed to discover in the preacher an old friend whom he had last met at an Eastern ball. The change in his friend, the sermon, with the blessing of the Holy Spirit, soon resulted in John Fell's conversion. At the invitation of Benjamin Fell, David Combs crossed the river and preached to a large congregation at the Fell homestead. A few days later near Wheeling he was murdered by the Indians. His untimely death, so soon after he had preached to them, made a deep impression upon the congregation at "the Forks."[2] From Fell's Church, the old Methodist hive, from which have swarmed so many religious workers, went John Fell who, after serving in the itinerancy for a while, first married Miss Christina Beazell, descendant of one of the founders of Fell's Church, and following her death married Miss Elizabeth Meason, daughter of Colonel Isaac Meason, of Mount Braddock. Before his removal to Zanesville, Ohio, sometime after 1831, he was active as a local preacher in his community.

In 1788, as we have seen, the Pittsburgh Circuit was formed. From that date through eight years there seems to have been no change in the names or general plan of the circuits. In 1796, however, Greenfield Circuit was created from parts of Greene, Washington, and Fayette Counties. Its name appears in the appointments until 1800, when it vanishes to return in 1804 and to continue until 1812. James Smith, who was to render to Methodism long and creditable service, was assigned along with James Lattomus the responsibility of organizing the new circuit. Lattomus, who was a native of Newcastle County, Delaware, did not possess a constitution rugged enough to withstand the hardships of a circuit-rider's life. Eight years had exacted such a toll of strength that he was obliged to take a supernumerary relation in 1802, and in September, 1806, he passed to his reward.[3]

On the Ohio Circuit in 1796, with what divisions of time we are not told, served Shadrack John-

---

[2]Craig, Blanche, "The First Fifty Years of Fell's Church," pp. 8, 9. Miss Craig, of Tarentum, Pennsylvania, is a great-great-granddaughter of Benjamin Fell, one of the founders of the church which bears his name. For a very complete account of the beginnings of Methodism in Rostraver Township, Westmoreland County, and the surrounding country, see "The Old and New Monongahela" (Pittsburgh, 1893), by John S. Van Voorhis, M.D.

[3]See Minutes of the Annual Conferences (1773-1839), p. 146.

son, Jonathan Bateman, Andrew Nichols, and John Seward. With the exception of Andrew Nichols, who put ten years into the traveling ministry, the duration of the services of each of the above was comparatively brief. The appearance of the name of Nichols in 1796 as pastor of John Street Church, New York, and his appointment on Long Island, indicate that he must have ridden the Greenfield Circuit early that year. If such long transfers turn the thoughts of present-day church officials to the item of the preacher's moving expenses, one can set them at ease by reminding them that Henry Smith states that about this time he traveled from Chillicothe, Ohio, to a Conference in Baltimore at a cost of five dollars. Although the past is silent concerning Andrew Nichols as nearly a century and a half ago he moved along roads leading into Waynesburg and other points on the Greenfield Circuit, then as now, like the proverbial home-town boy, he seemed to be heard from upon his arrival in New York. An historian of Old John Street Church says: "The preachers stationed in New York in 1796 were George Roberts and Andrew Nichols. Mr. Nichols was an excellent man and a good pastor and preacher. I have heard the old Methodists speak highly of him. Some still remember him, although it is sixty-one years since he preached in New York. Mr. Nichols was ten years an itinerant minister, having joined in 1791 and located in 1804."[4]

In 1796 one of the most remarkable men of the first half-century of American Methodism was appointed to the Pittsburgh Circuit. He was William Beauchamp, son of a Methodist preacher of the same

---

[4]Wakeley, J. B., "Lost Chapters Recovered From the Early History of American Methodism," p. 485.

name, and was born in Kent County, Delaware, in 1772. When about sixteen years of age he moved with his parents to the present state of West Virginia. How he acquired his store of learning, which was so vast and so diversified as to place him in the first rank of Methodist scholars, seems difficult to understand. He went from the Pittsburgh Circuit to New York City, thence to New England, where in 1801, he was married to Mrs. Frances Russell, located, and resided on Nantucket until 1807, when he returned to Woods County, Virginia. To him belongs the distinction of publishing the first Methodist periodical, *The Western Christian Monitor*, at Chillicothe, Ohio, in 1816. His volume, "Essays on the Truth of the Christian Religion," which came from the press five years earlier, had already won him recognition as a theologian.

Due to marriage, ill health, and his embarkation upon special projects, his service in the itinerancy suffered frequent interruptions. In 1817, for instance, he left Chillicothe for Mount Carmel, Illinois, where, as leader of Methodist colonizers, he served as chaplain, surveyor of the town, schoolmaster, and physician. He experimented with chemistry, and Thomas S. Hinde, who knew him intimately, claimed that he "could build a house, make a clock, and repair watches."[5] He mastered Latin, acquired a fair knowledge of Greek, and left a manuscript volume, "Translations of Hebrew Texts With Comments." In 1824 he was elected a delegate to the General Conference, where he came within two votes of being elected to the episcopacy. William Beauchamp possessed real stature. In his day he was called "The Demosthenes of the West." He was not only elo-

---

[5] See memoir, "The Methodist Magazine," Volume VIII, pp. 17, 49, 86.

quent, but his writings reveal a mastery of English quite unusual for a Methodist minister of that day. And in spite of the fact that he dwelt in the rather rarefied atmosphere of the genius, he possessed balance, administrative ability, and those gentler qualities which made him strong in the affections of his friends. He seemed utterly indifferent to the honors of the church as he watched them approach and recede. Never robust, the Indiana District with its eleven circuits proved too much for him, and at only fifty-three years of age, he died in 1824 at Paoli, Orange County, Indiana. In William Beauchamp the versatile scholar, the eloquent preacher, and the polished gentleman, it can safely be said that in 1796 the Pittsburgh Circuit had a minister who could have filled with acceptability almost any pulpit in the land.

In 1796, the very year William Beauchamp was riding the Pittsburgh Circuit, the person who, thirty years later, was to conduct his funeral service, was living on his father's farm two or three miles from Ligonier, Pennsylvania. He was Robert R. Roberts, then a youth of eighteen, in whose father's home he had often heard the first itinerants preach. Ligonier had been an outpost where hearts had beat hard and fears had run high in the dramatic days of blockhouses, militia musters, and pioneer road-making. Young Roberts had been deeply impressed with occurrences in another field which to him were no less thrilling. There was Abel Fisher, of Quaker parentage who, having come under conviction through the plain preaching of a Methodist circuit-rider who had wandered into the neighborhood, at last unhitched his team in the field, mounted one of the horses, and rode off in pursuit of the preacher. Near Connellsville he overtook him and there in the Youghiogheny, as in the Jordan long ago, the sacrament of baptism brought him peace and sealed his vows of discipleship.

To a certain sunrise in May, on the top of the Allegheny Mountains, Bishop Roberts frequently looked back and of it said: "Until that morning my mind was not at rest. Then everything seemed changed. Nature wore a new aspect, as I arose and went to my work with cheerfulness." While William Beauchamp was going the rounds of his circuit in 1796, Robert Roberts was picking up the rudiments of an education under the tutelage of the Irish schoolmaster, McAbee, over in the home of Matthew Fisher, three and one-half miles from the Roberts' cabin. Roberts was the Daniel Boone of early Pennsylvania Methodists, although he had not that antipathy for society which is said to have caused the Kentucky pioneer to move still farther westward every time he heard that a plow had arrived in the neighborhood. His departure from his Ligonier home in 1796, his disappearance into the wilderness with bear trap, rifle, and scant provisions in a pack later to emerge on the Shenango in the present Mercer County, place him among the successors of the glorious company of "The Long Knives" of Boone's day. How in subsequent years he peddled his pelts in Greensburg, descended the Youghiogheny from Connellsville in a provision-laden piroque, and at Beaver followed the Beaver River, the Big and the Little Shenango Rivers to the settlement he had made, is an entrancing story of adventure and daring. In this narrative, however, we shall follow him to the home of Jacob Gurwell, a plain Irish local preacher of ordinary talents, but of extraordinary goodness. Neither there in his home on Chestnut Ridge, nor later as a neighbor in Mercer County, did Jacob Gurwell neglect an opportunity to direct young Roberts towards the path that led to the field of enlarged usefulness. In the company of those who further aided Roberts were Thomas McClelland, whose death while en route from Beaver County to Pittsburgh we have already noticed, and Thornton Fleming, who was the Presiding Elder of the Quarterly Conference that granted him a local preacher's license, and James Quinn, who later, while on the Little Shenango, induced him to enter the traveling ministry. These were some of the counsellors who helped Robert Richford Roberts out of his wilderness home into the ministry. In 1807 he was appointed pastor at Pittsburgh to which he had formerly come as hunter and trapper, and in 1816, having impressed himself upon the church through his superior gifts, he was elected to the episcopacy, the first married minister of Methodism to receive that office.

The slow and difficult ordeal through which the different religious bodies passed before work of a permanent nature could be established in Pittsburgh has already been noted. This tardiness was particularly true of Methodism. Eight years had passed since the Pittsburgh Circuit had been formed and Charles Conaway had included as a preaching place the settlement of log houses that nestled in the woods between the old garrison of Fort Pitt and Grant's Hill at the forks of the Ohio. The fact that in 1796, the year of which we are writing, only 198 members were reported for the entire Pittsburgh Circuit indicates with what discouraging slowness Methodist preachers saw their work proceed in the region in which Pittsburgh was included. In 1753, in his report to Governor Dinwiddie of an inspection of lands held by Virginia along the Ohio River, Major George Washington had written of the site where the Monongahela and Allegheny Rivers meet: "I spent some time in viewing the rivers and the land in the forks, which I think extremely well suited for a fort as it has absolute command of both rivers." Apparently the spot was better suited for forts than for churches. It seems that in this place where quite naturally we would expect to find the fullest traces of Methodist activities before 1796, we find the most meager. The name of Mrs. Mary Gaut, a widow who arrived in Pittsburgh from Ireland in 1784, to visit her brother, Thomas Wilson, has been preserved. The story of how through the influence of this aunt the three daughters of Thomas Wilson were converted, met regularly in services, which consisted of hymn singing, prayer, and the reading of one of John Wesley's sermons, has survived. Soon, however, the faithful few had moved to Sandy Creek, but not before they had entitled themselves to the claim of being the first followers of John Wesley and the first to conduct Methodist services in the village of Pittsburgh.

In 1796 there arrived in Pittsburgh to engage in business John Wrenshall. Almost from the hour of his appearance he devoted himself to the advancement of Methodism. He preached, provided a place for services, collected a congregation, extended hospitality to preachers, and became Bishop Asbury's chief counsellor and host in Pittsburgh. During the twenty-five years between his arrival in 1796 and his death in 1821, his interest in everything that pertained to Methodism in this region was sustained.

John Wrenshall was born in Preston, County of Lancaster, England, December 27, 1761, the oldest of twenty-one children. When a youth he went to Halifax where, while serving an apprenticeship in a business house, he became impressed with the earnestness of certain local Methodists. He formed a close friendship with Joshua Keighly, later an itinerant preacher. At nineteen years of age Wrenshall united with the Methodist society under the ministry of the venerable Alexander Mather, became a local preacher, and married Polly Bennington, a member of one of the bands. On a Sunday in 1794, Mr. and Mrs. Wrenshall arrived in Philadelphia with their five children. As soon as the boat docked Mr. Wrenshall started in search of John Dickins, Methodist Publishing Agent, for whom he had a package of letters sent from England. He found Dickins in a Methodist Church, became his guest for dinner, and received from him and his son such assistance as strangers needed.

Since the account given by John Wrenshall, not only of Methodism but of religion in general in Pittsburgh in 1796, is the most complete of that of any contemporary writer, and since it is probable that it has not heretofore appeared in print, we shall quote rather fully from his manuscript autobiography. It should be kept in mind that Wrenshall wrote in a day when the controversy between Calvinism and Arminianism was at its most merciless stage. It may be that our chronicler was intolerant not so much by nature as by nurture. He writes:

"After various difficulties, we arrived in Pittsburg the last week in July 1796. It was on Friday that we arrived, and put up at the sign of the Bear, where I had not been long ere I discovered that Seager, who had arrived about two hours before me, had communicated to Mrs. Postlewaite the landlady, and the rest of the boarders, that I was a methodist, and occasionally a Preacher. The next day, Saturday, I walked about through the Town, they were then engaged in building a new court house in the diamond, and one of the workmen attracted my attention on account of his steady attention to his business which was hewing stone, and the appearance of solidity. After some conversation, I asked him if there were any of the people call'd Methodists in the town? he reply'd that he knew not of any except one old man, whose name, and place of residence, he communicated to me, and I went in search of him. He appeared to be a man very low, in point of intelect, and equally so with respect to christian experience, so that I had little satisfaction from that quarter."

"On sunday morning after breakfast, I made inquiry about the meeting and was informed there was a Presbyterian and a German meeting in a direction that was pointed out to me. I went to the first, which was the nearest. It was built of logs. On entering it, I found the benches broken down and covered with dust. The pulpit too was covered with the same, and the whole exhibited evidences of haveing long since been deserted. While museing here, I perceived it was not totally abandoned, for besides myself, there were plenty of spiders, and the swallows were busily engaged in flying in and out of the broken windows, and the door, which had been left open on account of its decay'd or inferm state. . . . I went next to the German church, which was of Brick, but not half finished. I found the door, but haveing no steps to it, I was obliged to climb up, as well as I could, to enter. It had no floor but the joists were there, ready for one. On one of these, behind the door, I took my seat, and could not refrain from shedding a few tears at the desolate situation of the place, in point of religion. After a little time spent in silent prayer, I read a chapter or two, and remained there alone for about an hour, then returned to dinner."

"In the afternoon, my attention was attracted by a crowd which I discovered in the street. Bending my course thither, it proved to be a funeral procession attending a corps to the grave, which I joined and made one in the procession. Arriveing at the grave yard where the deserted church stood, at which I had been in the preceeding part of the day, I was somewhat surprized in observing that nothing was said to impress the minds of the liveing with the awfullness of this solemn change. Not having before seen so much indifference manifested, I asked a man that was standing by me if this was the manner in which they usually buried their dead. One of the bystanders instantly reply'd, in the Scotch, or broad Irish dialect, 'We never use any seremoney here.' This man, who was a rigid Covenanter, I afterwards knew, his manner of expressing himself, made an impression on my mind. It was Mark Deary, a man not much famed for sobriety, however he might be as a predestinarian. But although I might pitty I could not blame him, for if his creed was true, he could not help his want of temperance, seeing that whatsoever comes to pass was decreed so by the great creator and governour of all things—Wonderful absurdity!

"It was two weeks after my arrival, before the waggons came, during which I got a situation for opening, and made the necessary preparations. I brought with me from the rev. John McClosky of

St. Georges Church, a letter address'd to Peter Shiras, Esq. from Mount Holly in the State of New Jersey who owned that part of the Town where Fort Pitt and Fort Duquesne formerly stood, and was removing there with his family but had not yet arrived. In a few days, however, after I commenced, a venerable looking old gentleman called on me and very affectionately introduced himself as the aforesaid Mr. Shiras, who without ceremony pressed me to commence preaching, observing that he had no doubt but the Providence of God had directed both our courses thither, for the introduction of the gospel in Pittsburg. To this however, I beged to be excused for the present, but promised that when my family came which I had found necessary now to send for, I would assuredly comply with his request and with this he was satisfied. In the month of October 1796 my family arrived, concisting of my Wife and five daughters, and the old Gentleman immediately came and reminded me of my promise. Haveing now no plea, and possessing a disposition to do what good I could, I observed that if he would procure a place, and a congregation I was ready at any time he might designate. He therefore procured the use of the old unoccupy'd meeting house, gave notice to the inhabitants, and on the following sabbath day I preached for the first time to a crowded congregation, from the following words, 'Worship God.' The congregation was very attentive, composed of all descriptions of character. The Officers and soldiers from the Garrison marched in regular order to, and from the meeting, as persons ought on such occasions.

"The following sabbath day, I preached again to

a congregation larger than before, but did not finish my discourse. I therefore gave out that I would finish it by permission of the Almighty, on the succeeding Sabbath. My only motive for mentioning this circumstance so particularly is on account of the following result. When the sabbath arrived, and the hour of assembling came which was three in the afternoon, Mr. and Mrs. Shiras called on us to go to the meeting. On our arrival we found a large company including the soldiers parraded as before, among them, appearances of a tumult was discoverable. Enquireing into the cause, we were told by a person called Chambers, who was very much incensed that the Elders of the church had fixed padlocks on the door and gate and would not permit a free willer, alluding to me, to preach in their meeting house, and Mr. Chambers declared, having been a subscriber to the church, he would get an ax and cut the gate and door down, that I might finish my sermon. I requested him however, to be peaceable, to make no such attempt and immediately turned round and addressed the assembly to the following effect. 'Gentlemen and Ladies, I am sorry that it is not in my power to fulfill my engagement made to you on sunday last. I do not keep the key of this meeting house, but I do that of my own house. If therefore you will condescend to walk with me thither, I will sing a hymn, pray with you, and we will part in peace.' Immediately my wife and myself turned and walked slowly arm in arm, and Mr. and Mrs. Shiras did the same, walking by the side of us, and most of the company followed. Arrived at home, my Daughters and myself sung a hymn, after which I prayed and concluded, but the people unwilling to depart stood silently waiting for sometime till some one call'd out, 'Where will the next meeting be?' I answered, my house, you see, it is too small even for domestic use, much more is it so, for a meeting for public worship. Mr. Shiras then call'd out, and said, I have a large room in my house at the point, it is at your service at any time you please to accept it and while I have a house that is suitable for publick worship, it shall allways be open. I thanked him for his kindness, and gave out Preaching at the point, next Sabbath day, at three oclock in the afternoon. Thus ended the Calvinian, Dog and manger pollicy—and then commenced the regular preaching of the methodist society in this city of Pittsburg.

"At his house, we had preaching for about seven years, two thirds of which I had to fill up myself, except when business call'd me from home, in that case Mr. Shiras sung, prayed, and read one of Mr. Wesley's sermons or a chapter in the Bible, in which exercise, in my view, he excell'd, and conducted the meeting with much propriety. It may not be improper here to state, that several attempts had been made, previous to the arrival of Mr. Shiras and myself, to introduce the Preaching of a free salvation to all—for all and in all, that believe and obey, but with little success. For prejudice, bigotry, and sensuality, had so effectually enchained and blinded the minds of its inhabitants that it was call'd, 'A Sodom in miniature.' One of our Preachers of the name of Conway, and a Mr. Wesley Matthews, made the attempt but without success, at least permanently so. And the Revd Valentine Cook, had many difficulties to encounter. He stood, however, so firm, that by his wisdom, prudence, and piety, he withstood all the attacks of bigotry."[6]

This description of John Wrenshall's inability to find scarcely a vestige of a Methodist society in Pittsburgh indicates that all former efforts to establish a congregation had come to nought. The claim, therefore, that Mr. Wrenshall was the founder of Methodism in Pittsburgh seems entirely warranted. Sharing in this honor, as we have seen, was Peter Shiras, an early Pittsburgher of large business interests, but soon to return to his home in New Jersey. Fortunate it was that this old class-leader could put at the disposal of the newly arrived local preacher from England, a room for worship in historic old Fort Pitt. And significant, likewise, was the July day of 1796 when the Methodist merchant, John Wrenshall, arrived in Pittsburgh. A strong man had come over the mountains.

---

[6] Wrenshall, John, Manuscript "Autobiography," Volume III, pp. 29-39. The "Autobiography" of John Wrenshall consists of five neatly written and well-bound volumes. The last three contain comments on Pittsburgh Methodism between 1796 and 1817. Volume I contains this explanatory note: "These five volumes, written by John Wrenshall, were presented to me by his daughter, Mrs. Dent, the mother of Mrs. General Grant. They contain much valuable matter bearing on the early history of Methodism in Pittsburgh. (Signed) F. S. DeHass, Martins Ferry, Ohio, September 6, 1887." The first volume also contains an enclosure in the handwriting of Dr. Grafton T. Reynolds which in part reads: "When Gen. Frederick D. Grant presided at the lecture given by the late Bishop Newman at the General Conference in Cleveland in 1896, he prefaced his introduction of the lecturer by a reference to his Methodist ancestry, stating that his parents and grandparents were all Methodists. He could have gone back one generation beyond his grandparents and said that his mother's grandfather was a local minister of the Methodist Episcopal Church, and practically the founder of Methodism in a great city less than 150 miles from where he was speaking, his mother, Julia Dent Grant being the granddaughter of John Wrenshall." Dr. Reynolds states that the five volumes of Wrenshall's "Autobiography" were given by Mrs. Dent, grandmother of General Frederick Dent Grant, to Dr. DeHass, who shortly before his death turned them over to the Pittsburgh Conference Historical Society. They are now in the library of the Historical Society of Western Pennsylvania, Pittsburgh, Pennsylvania, which organization has generously agreed to serve as custodian for the Pittsburgh Conference Historical Society.

Chapter X

THE CURTAIN FALLS ON A CENTURY OF DRAMA

There are yet others to play their parts ere the curtain shall drop on the closing scene of that first century. Valentine Cook was returned as Presiding Elder of the district, to find that the fame of his forensic victory over at Congruity was still secure. The Wrenshalls were living on Market Street, Pittsburgh. To them another daughter, Emily, had been born, and soon thereafter they received a congratulatory note from the Reverend Valentine Cook. Its tone of felicity changed, however, as if the memories of the writer reverted from the joy in the Wrenshall home to the inhospitality the village had extended to him. He urged upon the newcomers "the necessity of watchfulness and prayer, because many burning and shining lights had been extinguished in Pittsburg."

In a short time Mr. Cook arrived in Pittsburgh and was a guest in the Wrenshall home. Of this visit Mr. Wrenshall has written as follows: "Over the store was a large room belonging to the tavern, and as the court of Allegheny County was sitting, this room was oft set apart for the grand Jury to dine, which was the case when the Rev. Valentine Cook paid us this visit. Dinner being ended, the foreman of the grand Jury, as was customary, began to be very loud and vociferous, stamping with his feet and danceing or cutting such capers as to compel the copper Teakettles suspended on hooks at the top of my store to join him in danceing till I was affraid they would fall on our heads. The Queensware on my shelves joined in the concert, and would have joined in the dance too, if we had not took them off the shelves to prevent it. This old hero of fun was one of those elders at the church who got padlocks to the gate and door of the church, lest it should be polluted by a free willer, by this an idea may be formed what kind of characters composed elders at that time, provided they were rich and influential. Now, mark the contrast — Mr. Cook stood, lost in amaze, at the folly and levity of men possessing wealth and influence, and who ought by virtue of their office, to be a terror to evil doers, and a praize to them that do well, but instead of this, were the ringleaders in folly."[1]

To the sensitive and guileless Valentine Cook, court time in the trading post of Pittsburgh was a little too much. When Mrs. Wrenshall came upon her guest, who had retired to an upstairs room, she found that the antics of the elder had driven the visitor to prayer. She quickly tiptoed out, "leaving him undisturbed as she found him, on his knees deeply engaged in prayer, with streaming eyes, imploring no doubt mercy for these thoughtless mortals and the interposition of heaven for our preservation."

James Quinn, who never failed to record a debate of those days, especially if Valentine Cook par-

---

[1] For the account of Cook's visit with Wrenshall in 1799, see Wrenshall's "Autobiography," Volume III, pp. 46-48.

ticipated, states that in this year of 1797 his champion met the Reverend John Corbly, "who was almost the oracle, and was regarded as the father of the Baptist Church" in Western Pennsylvania and Virginia. Mr. Quinn concedes that "it was conducted with ability on both sides." The subject of the debate was baptism. Half a century afterwards James Quinn, after paying a tribute to the Reverend John Corbly, expressed his satisfaction over recurring triumphs thus, "A few days since, I baptized two of the infant great-great-grandchildren of him who would not admit to the Lord's table one who had not been immersed by a Baptist minister upon a profession of faith."[2]

During the Conference year of 1797, James Smith served on the Redstone Circuit and with him was Solomon Harris, who brought his ministry of a decade to an inglorious end. That year the congregations on the Pittsburgh Circuit were benefited by the presence of Robert Manley, a preacher of unusual gifts. In response to the appeal from Reece Woolf, a local preacher who was always eager for the occupancy of needy fields, Bishop Asbury sent Mr. Manley to the Little Kanawha River the next year. While there he crossed over into Ohio and organized the first Methodist society in Marietta.[3] James B. Finley never forgot the first time he heard Robert Manley preach over on the Little Miami at a camp meeting at which Bishops Asbury and McKendree also were present. He refers to him as "a flaming herald of the cross, and pioneer of the Gospel in the West," and relates that shortly

---

[2] Wright, John F., "Sketches of the Life and Labors of James Quinn," pp. 217, 218.

[3] See Barker, J. M., "History of Ohio Methodism," pp. 94, 95.

A CENTURY OF DRAMA   131

after the meeting closed Manley became ill and was soon claimed by death.[4]

On the newly formed Greenfield Circuit James Paynter, long since forgotten, in 1797 held faithfully to the course he was to follow through forty-three years. And with him was William James, a probationer, who in striking contrast soon wearied of well-doing. Among preachers found west of the Allegheney Mountains in 1797 to whom, as to Paynter, was to be given length of years, was Nathanael B. Mills. As early as 1787, at the age of twenty-one, he followed the Methodist pathfinder, Anning Owen, into the Wyoming Valley, and fifty-eight years later he was still giving a faithful witness. At his death it was found that Mr. Mills, who had never married, had left his savings, his horse, saddle, and bridle to his brethren in the ministry.[5] Such was he with whom Jacob Colbert had the good fortune to serve on the Ohio Circuit in 1797.

During this year the travels of Bishop Asbury were greatly reduced, due to illness of such an alarming nature that for long periods his recovery was doubtful. He was, therefore, prevented from visiting his preachers beyond the Allegheny Mountains. Yellow fever was raging in the larger cities that year, which necessitated the transfer of the Conference from Philadelphia to Duck Creek, Delaware, and to change, as a preventive measure, several Conference sessions from autumn to spring. It was not without alarm that the preachers ventured into Baltimore on October 21, where the Conference convened in the newly erected Light Street

[4] See Finley, James B., "Autobiography," pp. 228, 229.

[5] See Armstrong, James Edward, "History of the Old Baltimore Conference" (Baltimore, 1907), pp. 106, 277, 278.

Church, destroyed by fire eleven months before. Of that Conference, Bishop Asbury makes the laconic observation, "There was great peace, and all the preachers, but myself, satisfied with their stations."

The year 1798 brought no changes in the personnel of preachers in this region other than the appearance of Edmund Wayman, a Marylander, who was sent to assist Jacob Colbert on the Redstone Circuit. His health, which was never equal to the exactions of the itinerancy, soon failed and he died in 1802. During the year John Dickins, whose hospitality to John Wrenshall in Philadelphia we have noticed, died of yellow fever, which caused Jesse Lee to record in his "History of the Methodists," "His death was more sensibly felt by the Methodist connection in general than we had ever known or felt in the death of any other preacher that had died among us."

The year 1799 found Mr. Hitt continued as Presiding Elder of the district, which extended over portions of three States. On June 29 the Pittsburgh Quarterly Meeting granted a local preacher's license to John Wrenshall, signed by Daniel Hitt. Mr. Wrenshall had made an extensive business journey by boat to the Southern cities which had taken him from Pittsburgh from November, 1798, to the latter part of April, 1799. His interest in the promotion of Methodism never flagged. Indeed when the boat was detained, due to the death of an Irish sailor who fell overboard as a result of too much liquor at his farewell parties, Wrenshall revealed his inclination to let no opportunity, howsoever tragically produced, go unimproved. He wrote: "This specimen of intemperance and its dreadful effects, detained us some time longer because he had to be buried, while

I gladly embraced the interval, in visiting my family once more, and once more preached to the little society assembled at the point on Sunday from the following words 'See that ye forsake not the assemblying of yourselves together as the custom of some is.' It was a comfortable time."[6]

No sooner had John Wrenshall returned from his trip in the spring of 1799 than he was again planning for the two interests that lay nearest to his heart. He mentions his family, consisting of his wife and six daughters, "and the care of the little flock which mett every Sabbath day at the point, and which had unavoidedly been somewhat neglected during my absence and took up all my leisure time."[7]

Mr. Wrenshall follows this declaration of purpose with a description of the lack of Methodist activities in Pittsburgh in 1799, which in the light of the Church having sent preachers there for over a decade seems almost unbelievable. He writes: "The itinerant preachers in our connexion only pretended to visit Pittsburgh at that time one Sabbath day in two weeks. And what with quarterly meetings, which they attended; and high waters; we were frequently four and six weeks, and none but myself and Peter Shiras, Esquire, to fill up the appointments. I had to insist on Mr. Shiras filling up one vacancy out of three, as a relief for the congregation as well as myself; in which, in my view, he was well quallified, for although he did not pretend to preach, his juditiouse selection of Mr. Wesley's sermons, which he often read, and his pointed exhortations and devout prayers, were of great useful-

---

[6] Wrenshall, John, Manuscript, "Autobiography," Volume III, p. 52.
[7] Wrenshall, John, Manuscript, "Autobiography," Volume IV, p. 110.

ness in keeping up something like regular Christian worship in this place. These objects, therefore, that is, my business, my family, and the keeping up of a regular course of public and family worship agreeable to the best light I had and in proportion as my family increased, fully occupied my mind."

The preachers who were sent to their appointments in 1799 were for the most part changed from adjoining circuits. Charles Burgoon, who was the junior preacher on the Redstone Circuit with James Paynter this year, received his first introduction to Western Pennsylvania. "Worn out with pain" is the description given of his body by the writer who described his death, which occurred in 1800. When Henry Smith was engaged in writing his "Recollections and Reflections of an Old Itinerant" at Pilgrim's Rest, he referred to Charles Burgoon as he came down to the day of his death in Maryland, the State of his nativity. Smith said, "They buried him in the grave-yard, not three hundred yards from where I am writing, but no one can point out his grave with any certainty."

To the Greenfield Circuit with Edmund Wayman went James Quinn in 1799. John Quinn, who had arrived in the neighborhood of Canonsburg with Colonel Canon, married Sarah Henthorn, whose parents were living near Uniontown when Braddock was defeated. To John and Sarah Quinn was born in 1775 a son, James, who more nearly than any other person literally grew up with Methodism in Western Pennsylvania. We have already seen how as a lad with eyes big with wonder he watched Bishop Asbury in gown and band officiate at the ordination of Michael Leard in Uniontown in 1788, the first to take place west of the Allegheny Mountains. Forty years after he had risen from a chest behind a door to go forward to unite with the Church in the home of Colonel Beck, he returned to be shown that same chest by Mrs. Beck, the aged widow of the Colonel.*

From the home of William Wilson, a local preacher and quite likely an instructor in the Union School, Uniontown, James Quinn rode away in 1799 to his first appointment, the Greenfield Circuit. From that obscure beginning he moved outward and upward until his paths led him as a Presiding Elder over districts for twelve years, around circuits for twenty-two, and up to eight General Conferences. Few men so successfully repudiated the old adage about a prophet being without honor in his own country as did James Quinn, who was born in Washington County and was reared in Fayette County. In 1847 he was laid to rest in the churchyard of Auburn Chapel, five miles north of Hillsboro, Ohio. Jesse Stoneman, once the beloved class-leader in the neighborhood of Colonel Beck, whose influence extended to Kadesh Chapel, the West Liberty, Short Creek, and Pierce Run communities, joined the ranks of the traveling ministry to be sent to the Ohio Circuit in 1799.

*The home of Colonel John Beck, favorite stopping place of Bishops Asbury and Whatcoat, and widely known through the Redstone Country as a meeting place of the early Methodists, stood on a hillside facing Long Run three miles east of West Liberty, Ohio County, West Virginia. Many years ago the great house that had sheltered so many itinerants and witnessed so many Pentecostal awakenings, burned. Less than one hundred yards distant from the site of the house is the family burying ground overgrown with brambles, and with the tombstones fallen over. Deeply imbedded in an ancient tree is the slab of Colonel Beck. And near by is the overturned headstone of Simon Lauck, a notable early itinerant, whose second wife was the daughter of Colonel and Mrs. Beck. The crude headstones that mark the graves of the slaves extend into an adjoining range for swine. There is a tradition that the Colonel decreed that no fence should ever separate the plots in which he and his slaves should eventually rest. To the home of Colonel Beck Henry Boehm came with Bishop Asbury, and there on a tree on August 30, 1810, carved his name, and fifty years later sighed, "But where is our host, his family and his guests?" The springhouse to which the thirsty circuit-rider repaired, a pear tree of questionable antiquity and the neglected burying ground where Colonel Beck and Simon Lauck sleep among their kinsmen, are among the landmarks on this farm which is now owned by Charles Stanley Sonda.

There are hardships that wear away some enthusiasms and barriers before which the weak of will come to a halt. The glory of the circuit-riders who first scaled the Allegheny Mountains and moved along the dim trails to the cabins of the settlers, does not rest upon the claim that none turned back, but rather upon the record that so many held steadfastly to the way. From the earliest days when Robert Wooster, Reason Pumphrey, and Eli Shickle offered their testimonies before the pioneer congregations until the year 1800, when strong men like Daniel Hitt, Valentine Cook, and James Quinn had arrived to extend their brave witness, the story is one of patient endurance.

INDEX

Abbot, Benjamin.......... 18
Abingdon, Maryland....... 49
Alleghany Circuit 21
Allegheny County 71
Allison, Francis.......... 27
Angers, John............. 40
Arnold, George........... 91
Asbury, Francis...........
  biographical sketch, 21, 22; first visit to Western Pennsylvania, 22; meets Coke and Whatcoat at Barratt's Chapel, 39; ordination at Christmas Conference, 40; comment on Wilson Lee's death, 48, 49; first Uniontown Conference, 58-61; first visit to Pittsburgh, 70; second Uniontown Conference, 73; comment on John Wesley's death, 78; his will 93
Asbury's Journals........ 69
Ayres, Robert............ 50

Baltimore 43, 45, 52, 59, 68, 69
Banning, Anthony..33, 75, 89
Barker, John Marshall.... 75
Barratt's Chapel.......... 39
Bascom, Henry B......... 85
Bateman, Jonathan........ 115
Beatty, Charles........... 27
Beauchamp, William...116, 117
Beaver, Pennsylvania...26, 66
Beazell, Christina......... 114

Beck, John........31, 79, 135
Beeson, Henry.........23, 84
Beesentown (Uniontown), 23, 49, 51
Bell, Thomas............. 96
Berlin, Pennsylvania...... 67
Bethel Academy.......... 91
Boardman, Richard.....18, 19
Bodystone, Mrs........... 23
Boehm, Henry.........18, 85
Boehm, Martin........... 19
Bonham, Hezekiah..22, 23, 99
Bonham, Robert.......... 99
Boquet, Col. Henry....... 24
Boydston, David.......... 38
Boydston, George......... 38
Braddock, General........ 15
Breeze, Samuel..13, 15-19, 21, 25, 27, 29, 30, 32, 37, 38, 43-45, 66, 111
Broad Ford.............. 36
Brownsville ..24, 28, 33, 66, 95
Burd, Fort............... 24
Burd, Col. James......24, 27
Burgoon, Charles........ 134
Burke, William.........19, 98
Bunn, Seely 91, 92, 96

Callahan, George....61, 74, 75
Cann, Robert............. 61
Canonsburg, Pennsylvania, 37, 66
Carroll, Thomas.......... 68
Cartwright, Peter......47, 64
Casner, Mrs.............. 113
Chalfant, Chads.......... 33
Chaplin, John............ 33

137

INDEX

Chaplin, Thomas.......... 33
Charlestown, West Virginia, 99
Cheuvront, Joseph........ 65
Christmas Conference ..40, 54
Clarksburg, West Virginia,
    58, 77
Clarksburg Circuit,
    61, 65, 100, 103
Coke, Bishop Thomas,
    39, 40, 43, 52, 59, 109
Cokesbury College......49, 108
Colbert, Jacob.......131, 132
Coleman, James.......... 78
Combs, David............ 113
Conaway, Charles..61, 63,
    68, 71, 74, 75, 79, 83, 84,
    96, 100, 109, 113
Conferences at Uniontown,
    1788 58
    1790 73
    1792 ....81, 87
    1794 99
    1796 112
Confluence, Pennsylvania.. 67
Congruity Congregation... 88
Connell, Mrs. Zachariah,
    68, 105, 106, 112
Connellsville, Pennsylvania,
    66, 68, 71; Quarterly Conferences at............. 33
Cook, Valentine..19, 88-91,
    94, 108, 126, 128, 129, 136
Cooper, Ezekiel........... 33
Cooper, John..13, 15-21, 25,
    27, 29, 30, 32, 37, 38, 43-
    45, 66, 111
Corbly, John 27, 130
Coxe's Fort............... 51
Crawford, Joseph......... 45
Cresap, Col. Jacob.....24, 48
Croghan, George.......... 26
Cromwell, Joseph.......53, 61

Davies, Jane............. 95
Davis, Hanover........... 70
Deakins, Stephan......... 50
Dean, Henry Clay........ 86
De Hass, F. S............ 127
Dickins, John......17, 109, 132
Dodd, Thaddeus.......... 28
Doddridge's Chapel....... 76
Doddridge's Fort....51, 61, 66
Doddridge, John........37, 76
Doddridge, Joseph..37, 60, 75
Dunlap, James........... 28
Durbin, John P........... 35

Elliott, Charles........... 85
Everett, Joseph........... 17

Fell, Benjamin.........66, 113
Fell John.........33, 113, 114
Fell's Church.........102, 114
Ferguson, Richard......33, 102
Fidler, Daniel..........77, 78
Fidler, John........44, 46, 49
Finley, James B.......27, 130
Fisher, Abel.............. 117
Fleming, Thornton........ 119
Foot, John............... 33
Foster, Thomas........44, 49
Frazier, George........... 37

Garrettson, Freeborn,
    19, 44, 46, 52, 82
Gatch, Phillip..........19, 20
Gaut, Mrs. Mary.......... 120
Gist, Christopher......... 26
Grant, Julia Dent......... 127
Green, Lemuel......68, 69, 71
Greenfield Circuit.....114, 131
Greensburg, Pennsylvania. 70
Gurwell, Jacob........118, 119

Hadden, James........... 83
Hall, Joseph.............. 71

INDEX 139

Hamilton, Alexander...... 100
Hannastown, Pennsylvania,
    18, 70
Hardie, Thomas............ 29
Hardin, Col. John......95, 96
Harris, Solomon.......... 130
Haw, James............14, 30
Hawkins, Thomas......... 36
Hawkind, William......... 36
Haymond, Thomas.77, 103, 104
Henthorn, Mary.......... 90
Higgins, James L........ 113
Hite, Col. John........... 56
Hitt, Daniel....91, 93, 94,
  101, 109, 112, 113, 132, 136
Hitt, Herman..........93, 97
Hitt, Martin.............. 93
Hitt, Samuel............. 93
Hitt, William............. 93
Hollingsworth, Ann....... 68
How, William............ 36
Hunter, William.......... 86

James, William........... 131
Jamison, John........89, 90
Jarratt, Devereaux........ 14
Jennings, David.......... 36
Johnson, Shadrack........ 114
Jones, Greenbury R....... 33
Jones, John.............. 32

Kadesh Chapel........77, 135
Kennedy, James.......... 62
King, Enos............... 67
King, Michael............ 67

Lackey, F............37, 57
Lakin, Benjamin.......... 34
Lattomus, James........ 114
Lauck, Simon............ 135
Leard, Michael.....59, 60, 134

Lee, Jesse....18, 19, 60, 74,
    92, 100, 109
Lee, John................ 46
Lee, Wilson..44-49, 63, 80, 98
Light Street Church...... 109
Ligonier, Pennsylvania..18, 55
Ligonier Valley........... 67
Lincoln, Abraham......86, 93
Lucas, Thomas........... 92
Lunsford, Isaac........74, 92
Lurton, Jacob..63, 64, 67,
    68, 92
Lyell, Thomas............ 108

Madison College........84, 85
Manley, Robert........... 130
Martin's Church.......... 38
Matson, Enoch........... 50
Matthews, Lasley....63-65,
    67, 68, 92
Meason, Elizabeth........ 114
Meason, Col. Isaac....107, 114
Meason, Thomas.......... 107
Mills, Nathaniel B........ 131
Monongahela District..... 94
Montour, Andrew.......26, 27
Moore, D................. 67
Moore, Thomas........... 71
Morgantown, West Virginia,
    38, 49
Moriarty, Peter....17, 44,
    45, 46, 49
Muhlenberg, Frederick A.. 26
Muhlenberg, Henry Melchoir 26
Muhlenberg, John Peter Gabriel 26
Murphy, Mrs. Ann.....36, 107
Murphy, Jacob........... 107
McClelland, Thomas....... 34
McClelland, William...... 33
McDowell, William........ 56

INDEX

McKeesport, Pennsylvania, 66
McKendree, Bishop William 83
McLean, A............... 67
McLenahan, William...... 79
McMillan, John.......... 28

Necessity, Fort.......... 26
Neely, Bishop Thomas B.. 52
Neville, General John...... 100
Newland, George.......... 37
Nichols, Andrew.......... 115

O'Cull, James............ 34
Ohio Circuit....65, 66, 77, 79, 92, 97, 100, 131, 135
Ohio Company............ 24
O'Kelley, James........21, 39
Old Town, Maryland.24, 48, 96
Otterbein, Bishop......... 19
Owen, Anning............ 131

Parker, Samuel........... 64
Paynter, James........... 131
Pearson, Richard....61, 66, 68
Peck, Jacob............87, 88
Pedicord, Caleb........17, 20
Phelphs, Elisha.....53, 55, 56, 61, 99
Phillips, John............. 101
Phoebus, William....53-55, 58, 60, 61
Pike Run..............37, 66
Pilmoor, Joseph........18, 19
Pitt, Fort..............18, 28
Pittsburgh, Pennsylvania, 62, 70, 71, 127
Pittsburgh Circuit..61, 65, 75, 79, 88, 91, 100, 103, 110, 114, 119
Porter, Samuel......88, 90, 91
Post, Charles Christian.... 26

Poythress, Francis, 14, 17, 30, 98
Pumphrey, Caleb......... 77
Pumphrey, Reason..30, 31, 136
Putnam, General Rufus... 71

Quinn, James....21, 32, 33, 45, 50, 55, 56, 59, 66, 67, 77, 79, 90, 97, 107, 129, 134-136
Quinn, John.............. 134

Randolph Circuit.......... 75
Redstone Circuit...13, 24, 76-78, 87, 92, 96, 100, 103, 113
Redstone Creek........... 84
Redstone Old Fort.....24, 51
Reed, Nelson............. 17
Reiley, Abigail............ 67
Reiley, Cornelius.......... 67
Reiley, James......67, 87, 88
Reiley, Tobias............ 67
Reynolds, John H....103, 106, 107
Riggs, Jeremiah.......... 36
Riggs, William............ 37
Robbins, Isaac............ 65
Roberts, Benjamin......14, 30
Roberts Chapel........38, 52
Roberts, Robert R..34, 55, 67, 89, 105, 117-119

Scott, Thomas 97-99
Scull, John.............71, 81
Sebrell, Nicholas.......... 68
Seward, John............. 115
Shepherd's Meeting House. 37
Shepherd, William........ 37
Shewell, Henry........... 33
Shickle, Eli............31, 136
Shiras, Peter.....124, 125, 133
Simmons, John........... 68

INDEX 141

Simpson, Matthew........ 85
Smith, Henry..47, 101-106, 134
Smith, James........114, 130
Smith, John............50, 51
Smith, Joseph............ 28
Smith, Pemberton......... 68
Snethen, Nicholas......... 39
Solomon, John............ 67
Somerfield, Pennsylvania, 15, 67
Somerset County.......... 67
Spahr, Thomas........... 77
Stoneman, Jesse.......... 135
Strawbridge, Robert, 18, 22, 31, 39, 99
Sutton, John............. 27

Taylor Church..34, 36, 37, 48, 64, 66
Taylor, Joseph............ 48
Thompson, Amos G., 77, 78, 87
Thrift, Minton............ 75
Tiffin, Edward............ 99
Todd, John............... 66
Tomlinson, Henry......... 33
Trent, Captain............ 24
Tucker, Samuel........... 34

Union School......83, 107, 108
Uniontown (Beesontown) 23, 27, 32, 45, 48, 49, 52, 53, 58-60, 64, 66-68, 77, 81, 99, 113

Vasey, Thomas........... 39

Ware, Thomas......19, 20, 53
Washington, Pennsylvania, 48, 52, 66

Washington Circuit....... 100
Washington County 76, 94
Washington, George.24, 26, 38, 43, 120
Watson, John.....101, 102, 109
Wayman, Edmund........ 132
Waynesburg, Pennsylvania. 34
Weber, Johann Wilhelm... 28
Webster, Richard......... 18
Weiser, Conrad.........25, 26
Welsh, Reverend Mr...... 98
Wesley, Charles.......... 39
Wesley, John....17, 29, 30, 39, 40, 41, 52, 53, 59, 78
West Middletown, Pennsylvania 37, 66
West Newton, Pennsylvania 66, 71
Whatcoat, Richard..35, 39, 40, 52, 53, 55, 58-60, 69
Whisky Insurrection...... 100
White, Alward 97
White, Thomas........... 22
White Eyes, Chief........ 76
Whitefield, George........ 19
Williams, Robert.......... 17
Willis, Henry.......68, 69, 71
Wilson, James...53, 55, 57, 61
Wilson, Thomas.......... 120
Wilson, William........33, 107
Winans, William.......... 64
Woodfield, Daniel......... 34
Woodfield, Gabriel W...34, 64
Woodfield, Joseph......... 37
Wooster, Robert....32, 33, 136
Wrenshall, John........120-134
Wright, Richard.......... 22

Young, Jacob............. 76